PUNK KNITS

26 HOT NEW DESIGNS
FOR ANARCHISTIC SOULS AND INDEPENDENT SPIRITS

SHARE ROSS

Photographs by Bam Ross

STC CRAFT | A MELANIE FALICK BOOK

STEWART, TABORI & CHANG
NEW YORK

KNITTING? ME? NEVER!

That's what I would've said a couple of years ago. I'm a rock 'n' roller. Rockers don't knit. Even my friends said so. It just didn't seem like something I would ever get into. I've dabbled in painting and writing, but knitting? C'mon. That's for grannies.

I have since discovered that knitting is an amazing way to make a truly anarchistic statement, and in the process make some great clothing that reflects an independent spirit. What is more rock 'n' roll than making your own fashion statement and snubbing the corporate entities that tell us how to look?!

All that without having to learn how to sew.

It all started when a friend came over wearing a scarf she'd just made for herself. I totally flipped for it and when I asked her about it she said she'd knit it herself.

That was it.

Seeing is believing.

I taught myself using online tutorials. From there, it's developed into a full-blown habit. I mean addiction. I mean, suddenly I stare at every single sweater, scarf, hat, glove, etc., etc., etc., and drive my friends and family insane with my enthusiasm for yarns.

Welcome to my world!

Share Ross

THIS BOOK IS LOVINGLY DEDICATED TO A VERY TALENTED AND CHARISMATIC WOMAN, MY MOTHER, VERA J. HOWE (1929-2005), WHO BELIEVED I COULD DO ANYTHING I SET MY MIND TO AND ENCOURAGED ME TO PURSUE MY DREAMS.

Published in 2007 by Stewart, Tabori & Chang
An imprint of Harry N. Abrams, Inc.

Text copyright © 2007 by Share Ross
Photographs copyright © 2007 by Bam Ross

Ross, Share.
   Punk knits / Share Ross ; Photographs by Bam Ross.
       p. cm
   ISBN 1-58479-583-2
   1. Knitting. I. Title.
   TT820.R746 2007
   746.43'2--dc22
   2006017055

Editor: Melanie Falick
Designer: Noël Claro
Production Manager: Jacqueline Poirier

The text of this book was composed in Franklin Gothic and Chase.

Printed and bound in China
10 9 8 7 6 5 4 3 2 1

HNA ▌▌▌▌▌
harry n. abrams, inc.
a subsidiary of La Martinière Groupe

115 West 18th Street
New York, NY 10011
www.hnabooks.com

PUNK KNITS

WHY KNIT?

Knit because you want TO CREATE SOMETHING. Knit because you want TO GIVE SOMEONE A GARMENT YOU MADE for them. Knit because you want TO EXPRESS YOURSELF. Knit because you spend a ton of time on your computer and YOU FIND THE FEEL OF YARN VERY SOOTHING. Knit because IT CALMS YOU DOWN in an increasingly stressful world. Knit FOR YOUR OWN MULTITUDE OF REASONS that are unique to your life and your situation.

While I was working on this book, of course I talked about it a lot. And often the people I was talking to wanted to know what I thought was punk about knitting. So I pondered and, you know what? The more I thought about it, the more I began to wonder . . . what's NOT punk about knitting? Anybody can do it and it can be as artistic as you want it to be; you can make your own clothes and make a statement; and in your own personal way, you can snub the corporations that try to strip away your individuality by knitting garments instead of buying them.

But before you go and call your granny to say, "Hey, Grandma, you're PUNK!," please remember that punk knitting is a mindset, a lifestyle, and a way of thinking. While I believe that all knitters are punk for the very reasons set out here, your grandma may not appreciate the comparison. But let her know that I love her for pursuing a craft that leaves a legacy and a trail of beauty for generations to come.

And, for more answers to the question—What's so punk about knitting?—check out the quotes I collected from punk knitters around the country that are sprinkled throughout this book.

SO, REALLY, WHY KNIT? There are as many reasons to knit as there are yarns to knit with, so I'll just share a few of my favorites. For starters, it's easy and downright cool these days. There are only two stitches to learn, knit 'n' purl (sounds like rock 'n' roll, doesn't it?). Everything else you encounter is a variation of those two stitches. I can do them and I practically flunked home economics in school. So I'm convinced anyone can.

A second big reason is creativity—we knitters are a creative bunch! Our most basic source of satisfaction is derived from making something ourselves. Much like

RESOURCES FOR NEW KNITTERS

LEARNING TO KNIT FROM A BOOK

Stitch 'n' Bitch: The Knitter's Workbook
by Debbie Stoller
A super-fun and easy book to teach you all the basics and more.

Vogue Knitting: The Ultimate Knitting Book
by the Editors of Vogue Knitting
A thorough guide—not punk, but very helpful.

Knitting Without Tears
by Elizabeth Zimmermann
Zimmermann makes you feel like she's right there with you, and her knowledge is immense (plus she encourages knitters to make their own rules and patterns).

LEARNING TO KNIT ONLINE

Knittinghelp.com
www.knittinghelp.com

Fiberartshop.com
www.fiberartshop.com/knclbg.htm

ONLINE COMMUNITY RESOURCES

Revolutionary Knitting Circle
www.knitting.activist.ca
An activist group with excellent peace projects.

Punk Knitters at Live Journal
www.livejournal.com/community/punk_knitters/
A forum where like-minded anarchist knitters can post questions and guide each other.

Knitty
www.knitty.com
An online magazine full of patterns, tips, and lots of knitting info.

Punk Knits
www.punkknits.com
My Web site where I share extras and host a message board as well! Please join us.

Cast Off
www.castoff.info
A British knitting club with outrageous knitting kits in their online shop.

"Knitting can be very ordered...I OFTEN TURN MY RAMBLINGS OFF THE PATH (ACCIDENTS AND NOT FOLLOWING THE PATTERN!) into a feature or a benefit. One thing I like to say to my friends is 'What wouldn't my mother/granny do?' and then do it." -MARY D., SYDNEY, AUSTRALIA • CHECK OUT HER MOSH PIT CHOKER ON PAGE 54

is what I recommend to anyone who needs to learn the basic stuff and, like me, doesn't have a friend or family member to teach them. (But for those who are committed to learning from a book or online or just find themselves needing information in the middle of the night, I have gathered the list of resources at left). The first time I went to a proper LYS, I was intimidated by the fact that they didn't post their prices on any of the yarns, and the array of choices, quite frankly, overwhelmed me. This was not a good LYS for me. I didn't feel welcome there, so after making several mistake purchases, I finally started searching for another one. I did find a fantastic LYS for me and have since bonded with the owner and ALL of her employees! They helped me with this book and with practically every project I have dreamt up.

SO, YOU WANNA MAKE HOLES? Finally, even though this isn't a how-to-knit book, I feel compelled to offer you one how-to lesson and that's how to make holes—on purpose—because holes are such an important part of so many designs presented here. I use three techniques: controlled drop stitches, yarnover holes, and bind-off holes. So, check out the instructions that begin on page 14. Then, please, dive right into the pattern pages of *Punk Knits*, choose a project (check out the rating system on page 17 if you're not sure what you can handle), turn up the stereo, and have fun.

MAKING HOLES
(ON PURPOSE!)

Most of the time when you're knitting you avoid dropping stitches off your needles because when you do your knitting can unravel all the way down to the cast-on edge, often taking on the look of a ladder at the point where the stitch (or stitches) dropped off. But, when I knit my first design, I was desperate to find out how to drop stitches to create a ladder-like opening that wouldn't unravel completely; instead, the "ladder" of the dropped stitch would stop at a desired point. Finally, I discovered a method for creating a controlled drop stitch by adding a stitch using an m1 (make 1) increase at the spot where I want the bottom rung of the ladder to be. Then I knit as usual until I reach the row where I want the top rung of the ladder to be. At that point, I drop the stitch I added all the way down to the original m1. Check out the instructions at right.

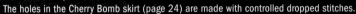
The holes in the Cherry Bomb skirt (page 24) are made with controlled dropped stitches.

14

CONTROLLED DROP STITCHES

INCREASE 1 WITH AN M1

Here are instructions for creating an m1 increase on the knit side of the fabric and on the purl side of the fabric.

Note: It is very important that you place the marker as instructed so that you will know where the m1 is located later when it's time to start dropping.

M1 KNIT SIDE

Step 1: Knit to the point where you want to add a stitch. Place a marker, then insert the left needle from front to back under the bar between the two needles and lift it onto your left needle.

Step 2: Knit the stitch you placed on your left needle through the back loop.

M1 PURL SIDE

Step 1: Place your marker, then insert the left needle from back to front under the bar between the two needles and lift it onto your left needle.

Step 2: Purl the stitch you placed on your left needle through the front loop.

DROP STITCHES ALL THE WAY DOWN TO THE M1

Step 1: When you have worked to the point where you want the top rung of your ladder to be, work to the marker, slip the marker to the right-hand needle, then, with the tip of your right needle, lift the next stitch on your left needle off the needle and drop it.

Step 2: Look at the little loop in between the two needles. This is the dropped stitch.

Step 3: Gently pull the two sides of the knitting apart so that the dropped stitch drops all the way down to the point at which you made the m1. In this photo, the m1 was 10 rows down, so there are 10 rungs on the ladder.

YARNOVER HOLES

A yarnover is a common technique in lace knitting. I like to make a few yarnovers in a row to create punk-style lace. On the Decon Sweater at right, the more triangular-looking holes are made with yarnovers.

Step 1: Work to the spot where you want the yarnover hole to start, then bring the yarn from the back to the front between the needles, then back down over the right needle.

Step 2: Make a second yarnover next to the first. Repeat as many times as you like.

Step 3: Knit the next stitch.

Step 4: Work the stitches in the next row as called for in your pattern (in this photo, they are purled), dropping the yarnovers off the needles without working them as you come to them.

BUTTONHOLE HOLES

This technique is conventionally used to make buttonholes, thus its name. At the spot where you want a hole, bind off the number of stitches desired (the more stitches, the bigger the hole). On the next row, work to the point where the bind-off stitches are located and then cast on the same number of stitches using the backward loop cast-on shown here or the method of your choice. On the Decon Sweater at right, the big oval holes are made this way.

BACKWARD LOOP CAST-ON

Step 1: At the spot where you need to begin replacing bound-off stitches, wrap yarn around left finger clockwise two times.

Step 2: Insert right needle into loop closest to end of finger and slip onto right needle.

Step 3: Gently pull on yarn to tighten new stitch on right needle.

The Decon Sweater (page 58) is made with both yarnover holes and buttonhole holes.

PUNK KNITS
RATING SYSTEM

If you're a new knitter and don't always know when you look at a *Punk Knits* pattern or picture how challenging the project might be, then use this rating system as a guide. But don't be afraid to try something new or different. Just take it one stitch at a time. Ultimately, there is only you, your ideas, and your yarn and needles. Follow the patterns in this book as written, or use them as starting points for your own ideas.

GARAGE
The Garage is where you start. This level is suitable for new knitters or folks who just want to do some easy, relaxing knitting.

COFFEE HOUSE
You've moved past the first level and you're ready for something more than scarves and rectangles. This level is great for advanced beginners.

NIGHTCLUB
Ahhh....the nightclub. These pieces might seem a little challenging to the absolute beginner. Or maybe they're simple pieces with a slightly new idea attached to them. Fun is the key word here.

THEATER
This level steps it up a notch to patient knitting and long patterns. This level can include colorwork.

ARENA
The big time! The Arena is for knitters who are ready for anything. Go for it!

THE GIG
26 PUNK PATTERNS

Motor City Arm Warmers (see page 118) and Madlad Hat (see page 74)

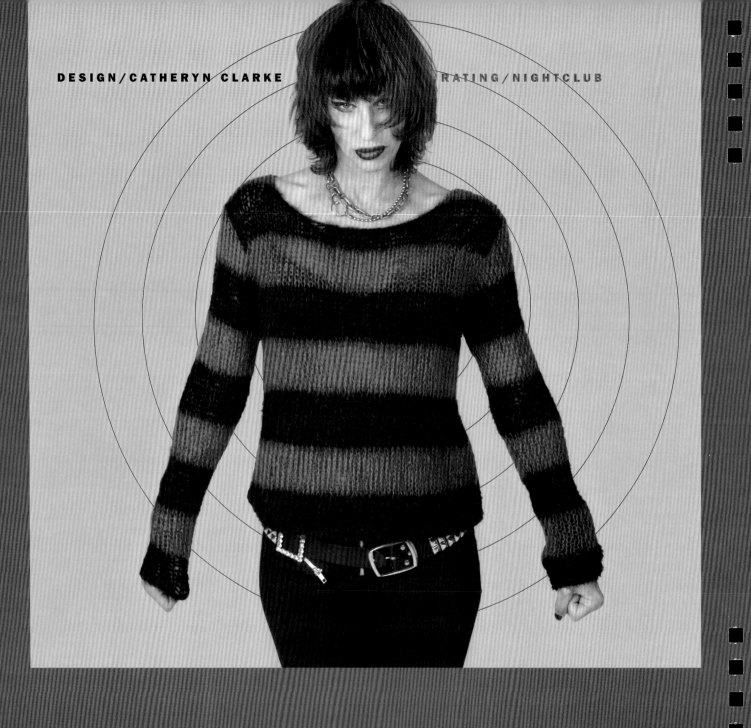

DESIGN/CATHERYN CLARKE RATING/NIGHTCLUB

1977 SWEATER

Forever über-hip, the **stripey sweater** is a stronghold in any punk's wardrobe—a timeless classic that hails back to the late '70s street style in London. This piece knits up **fast and furious** and can be worn by either gender. Please note: If you knit this for your boyfriend/girlfriend, you will want to borrow it because **it's so delicious to wear.** So, plan on making two!

INSPIRATION: SID VICIOUS

Along with Johnny, Steve, and Paul, The Sid and the Sex Pistols revolutionized music and fashion at the same time. They launched a style and sonic assault that shook the world.

SIZES
To fit bust/chest: 36 (42)"

FINISHED MEASUREMENTS
41 1/2 (49 1/2)" chest

MATERIALS
Yarn
Berroco Quest (100% nylon; 82 yards / 50 grams): 5 (8) skeins #9814 tuxedo (A)
Fonty Ombelle (70% kid mohair / 25% wool / 5% nylon; 157 yards / 50 grams): 2 (3) skeins #1019 hot pink (B)

Needles
One pair straight needles size US 13 (9mm)
Change needle size if necessary to obtain correct gauge.

GAUGE
10 sts and 13 rows = 4" (10 cm) in Stockinette stitch (St st) using either A or B

STRIPE SEQUENCE
Work 10 rows A, then 10 rows B.

SWEATER

BACK
Using A, CO 52 (62) sts. (RS) Begin St st and Stripe Sequence. Work even until piece measures 15 (16)" from the beginning, ending with a WS row.

SHAPE ARMHOLES
(RS) BO 3 sts at beginning of next 2 rows, then decrease 1 st each side every row 2 (4) times—42 (48) sts remain. Work even until armhole measures 5 (5 1/2)" from the beginning, ending with a WS row.

SHAPE NECK
K14 (16), join a second ball of yarn and BO center 14 (16) sts for neck, work to end—28 (32) sts remain. Working both sides at the same time, decrease 1 st each neck edge every row 4 times—10 (12) sts remain each side for shoulders. Work even until armhole measures 8 (9)". BO all sts.

FRONT
Work as for Back until armhole measures 4 (4 1/2)".

SHAPE NECK
K16 (18), join a second ball of yarn and BO center 10 (12) sts for neck, work to end—32 (36) sts remain. Working both sides at same time, decrease 1 st each neck edge every row 6 times—10 (12) sts remain each side for shoulders. Work even until piece measures same as for Back to shoulders. BO all sts.

SLEEVE (MAKE 2)

Using A, CO 21 (23) sts. Begin St st and Stripe Sequence. Work even for 10 rows.

SHAPE SLEEVE

Continuing in Stripe Sequence, increase 1 st each side this row, then every 10 (8) rows 5 (6) times as follows: K1, m1, work to last st, m1, k1—33 (37) sts. Work even until piece measures 19 (20)" from the beginning, ending with a WS row.

SHAPE CAP

BO 3 sts at beginning of next 2 rows, decrease 1 st each side every other row 0 (3) times, then every row 8 (6) times—11 (13) sts remain. BO all sts.

FINISHING

Block pieces to measurements. Sew shoulder seams. Set in Sleeves. Sew side and Sleeve seams. Weave in all loose ends.

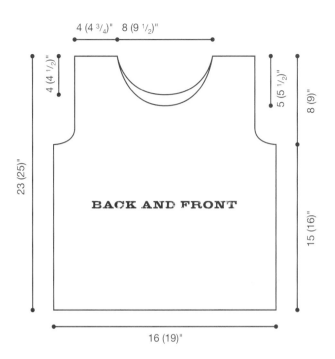

4 (4 3/4)" 8 (9 1/2)"

4 (4 1/2)"

5 (5 1/2)"

8 (9)"

23 (25)"

BACK AND FRONT

15 (16)"

16 (19)"

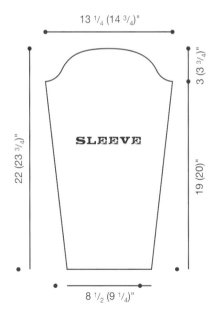

13 1/4 (14 3/4)"

3 (3 3/4)"

22 (23 3/4)"

SLEEVE

19 (20)"

8 1/2 (9 1/4)"

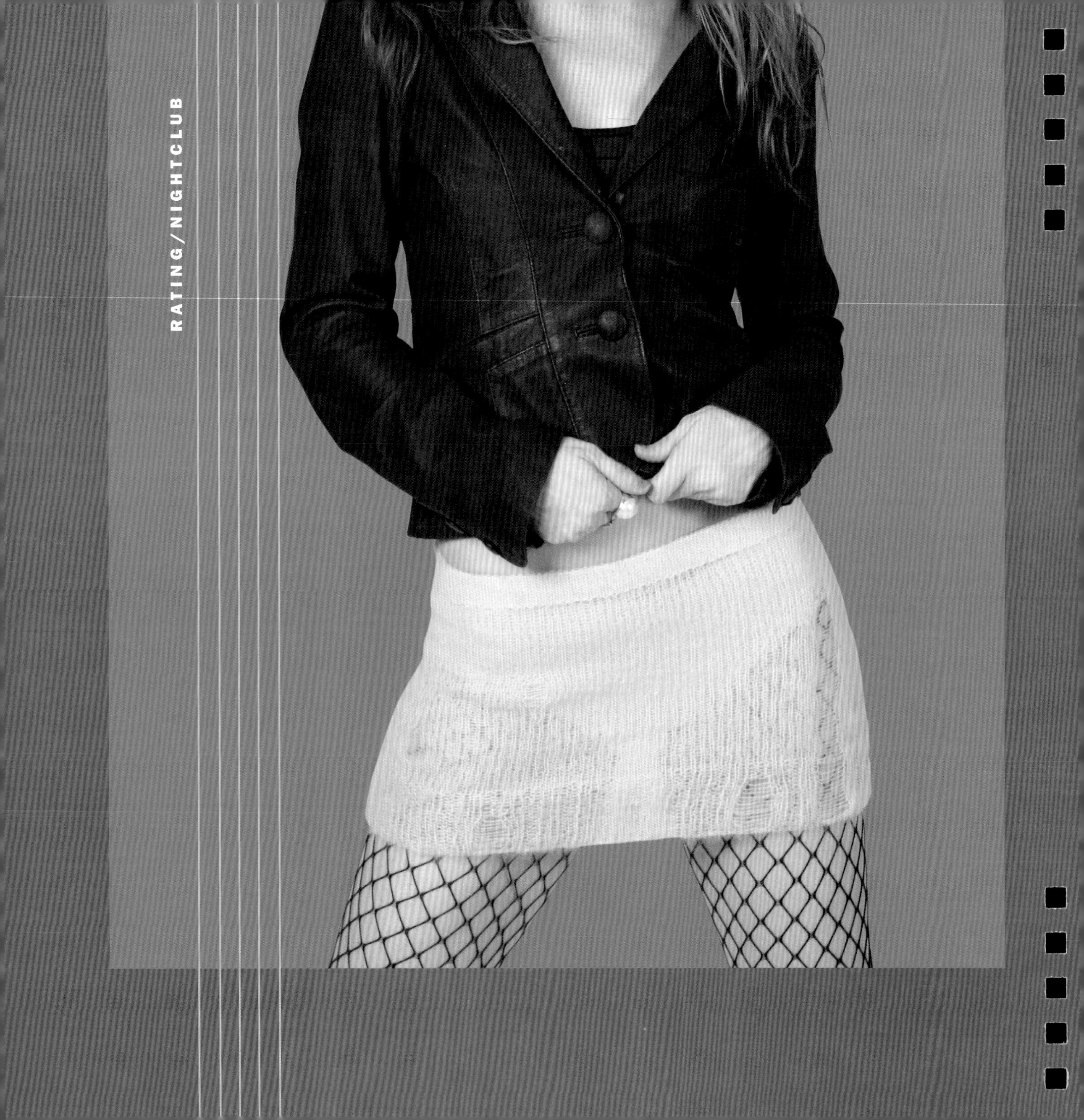
RATING/NIGHTCLUB

CHERRY BOMB

This little number is **super sheer, über sexy,** and only recommended

for the truly wild among you who don't mind being stared at. I paired

it with matching silky green panties and the required rocker black

fishnets, but you could easily wear this over jeans.

The thing is…**the yarn is so yummy soft,** you might want to keep it

close to your skin and go for the "sheer with knickers" look.

Using a combination of dropped stitches and "controlled" ladders, this

skirt is **ultra punk and ultra cool**.

INSPIRATION: THE RUNAWAYS

Chicks in rock owe a lot to the Runaways! Joan Jett, Lita Ford, and company
paved the way for many a girl to strap on a guitar and rock the house down.
Ch-ch-ch-cherry bomb! If you wear this skirt, you ARE a cherry bomb.

SIZES

To fit 32 (36, 39, 43, 46)" hip

FINISHED MEASUREMENTS

28 3/4 (32 3/4, 35 1/4, 38 3/4, 42)" hip (unstretched)
32 (36, 39, 43, 46)" hip (stretched)
24 3/4 (28 3/4, 31 1/4, 34 3/4, 38)" waist (unstretched)
27 (32, 34, 38, 42)" waist (stretched)
13 1/4 (13 3/4, 14 1/4, 14 3/4, 15 1/4)" length, including finished waistband
Skirt is very close fitting; consider this when choosing size.

MATERIALS

Yarn

Filatura Di Crosa Baby Kid Extra (80% super kid mohair / 20% nylon; 268 yards / 25 grams): 2 (3, 4, 5, 6) balls #478 lime green

Needles

One 29" (74 cm) circular (circ) needle size US 5 (3.75 mm) Change needle size if necessary to obtain correct gauge.

Notions

Stitch markers (6, in different colors); one yard 1"-wide non-rolling elastic; sewing needle and thread

GAUGE

19 sts and 28 rnds = 4" (10 cm) in Stockinette stitch (St st) using two strands of yarn held together

2X2 RIB

(multiple of 4 sts; 1-rnd repeat)
All Rnds: *K2, p2; repeat from * to end.

NOTES

This Skirt is knit entirely in the round.

"Controlled" ladders are formed by working m1 increases, which are dropped in later rounds. Ladders will be unraveled down to the point where the m1 was worked.

SKIRT

Using 2 strands of yarn held together, CO 68 (78, 84, 92, 100) sts, place marker (pm) for center of rnd, CO 68 (78, 84, 92, 100) sts—136 (156, 168, 184, 200) sts. Join for working in the rnd, being careful not to twist sts; pm for beginning of rnd. Begin 2x2 Rib. (Work even until piece measures 3" from the beginning.)

ESTABLISH DROPPED STITCHES

Note: Unravel all dropped sts down to CO row.
Drop Rnd 1: Continuing in pattern as established, work 50 (58, 62, 70, 74) sts, drop next st, CO 1 st, work to last 14 (14, 16, 18, 20) sts, drop next st, CO 1 st, work to end. Work even for 3 rnds.
Drop Rnd 2: Work 22 (26, 26, 30, 30) sts, drop next st, CO 1 st, work to end. Work even for 2 rnds.
Drop Rnd 3: Work 52 (56, 64, 72, 76) sts, drop next st, CO 1 st, work to end. Work even until piece measures 3 (3, 3 1/4, 3 1/2, 4)" from the beginning.

ESTABLISH LADDERS

Note: Unravel all Ladders to their respective m1 sts.
Change to St st. Work even until piece measures 4" from the beginning.
Ladder Setup Rnd 1: K8 (9, 10, 11, 12), pm for Ladder 1, m1, knit to 7 (8, 9, 10, 11) sts before center marker, pm for Ladder 2, m1, knit to end—138 (158, 170, 186, 202) sts. Work even for 6 rnds.
Ladder Setup Rnd 2: Knit to center marker, k11 (12, 13,

15, 16), pm for Ladder 3, m1, knit to 14 (15, 16, 18, 20) sts before end, pm for Ladder 4, m1, knit to end—140 (160, 172, 188, 204) sts. Work even for 2 rnds.
Ladder Rnd 3: Work to marker for Ladder 1, remove marker, drop next st; repeat for Ladder 2—138 (158, 170, 186, 202) sts remain. Work even for 3 rnds. (Piece should measure approximately 6" from the beginning.)

SHAPE SKIRT

Rnd 1 (Dec Rnd): K2tog, knit to center marker, k2tog, knit to end—136 (156, 168, 184, 200) sts remain.
Repeat Dec Rnd every 5 rnds 8 times, and AT THE SAME TIME, work Ladders on the following rnds:

Rnd 4: Work to marker for Ladder 3, remove marker, drop next st, work to end.
Rnd 8: Work to marker for Ladder 4, remove marker, drop next st, work to end.
Rnd 12: Knit to 20 (22, 25, 27, 30) sts before center marker, pm for Ladder 5, m1, knit to end.
Rnd 15: Knit to 20 (22, 25, 27, 30) sts after center marker, pm for Ladder 6, m1, knit to end.
Rnd 22: Work to marker for Ladder 5, remove marker, drop next st, work to end.
Rnd 25: Work to marker for Ladder 6, remove marker, drop next st, work to end.

Continuing decreases as established, work even in St st until Skirt measures 12 (12 1/2, 13, 13 1/2, 14)" or desired length to Waistband from the beginning—118 (138, 150, 166, 182) sts remain after all decreases are complete.

WAISTBAND

P6 (14, 22, 30, 38), drop next st, purl to end—117 (137, 149, 165, 181) sts remain. Work even for 8 rnds.
Purl 1 rnd (turning rnd). Work even for 8 rnds. BO all sts.

FINISHING

Measure your waist. Cut length of elastic 2" shorter than waist measurement and sew ends together. Fold Waistband over elastic to WS at turning rnd. Sew BO edge to WS of Skirt, being careful not to let sts show on RS. Weave in all ends.

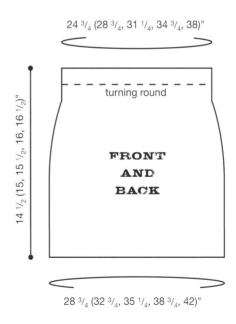

24 3/4 (28 3/4, 31 1/4, 34 3/4, 38)"

turning round

14 1/2 (15, 15 1/2, 16, 16 1/2)"

FRONT AND BACK

28 3/4 (32 3/4, 35 1/4, 38 3/4, 42)"

MOD GLOVES

When I first started knitting, I was desperate to make some fingerless gloves that didn't require anything "fancy" like double-pointed or circular needles. **This pattern is the bomb!** Using ribbing on both the bottom and top keeps the gloves from curling where you don't want a curl. Fingerless gloves are definitely **the knitted item my punk rock pals request most,** so have fun and make a bunch!

SIZES
Small/Medium (Large)

FINISHED MEASUREMENTS
6 1/2 (7 1/2)" circumference

MATERIALS
Yarn
Cascade Yarns 220 Superwash (100% washable merino wool; 220 yards / 100 grams): 1 ball #851 celery (A); Berroco Quest Colors (100% nylon; 82 yards / 50 grams): 1 ball #9934 pierrot (B)

Needles
One pair straight needles size US 9 (5.5 mm)
Change needle size if necessary to obtain correct gauge.

GAUGE
18 sts and 22 rows = 4" (10 cm) in Stockinette st (St st) using A, unstretched

NOTES
Gloves will appear small but will stretch once you put them on.

2x2 RIB
(multiple of 4 sts; 1-row repeat)
All Rows: K2, p2; repeat from * across.

Depending on the color of yarns you choose, **THESE CAN BE AS LOUD AS YOU WANT.** Go with more subtle color choices and you have a gentler, quieter pair of gloves.

GLOVES

Using one strand each of A and B held together, CO 24 (28) sts. Begin 2x2 Rib. Work even until piece measures 2 (2 1/2)" from the beginning.

Continuing in A only, change to St st. Work even until piece measures 4 1/2 (5 1/2)" from the beginning, ending with a WS row. Change to 2x2 Rib. Work even until piece measures 5 1/2 (7)" from the beginning, ending with a WS row. BO all sts in pattern.

FINISHING
Sew side seam, leaving a gap for thumb approximately 1 1/2 (2)" from BO edge. Make sure the gap is big enough for your thumb to pass through comfortably. Using yarn needle, weave in all ends.
Make second Glove to match first.

"I'M A BIG FAN OF CREATING YOUR OWN LOOK. Knitting my own kick-ass clothing is just the next step after combing Goodwill for an awesome shirt or pair of pants. It's also a great way to get clothes you might see advertised at mainstream department stores without having to pay obscene amounts of money." —SARAH K., HERNDON, VA

"Creating from your heart and MAKING UP THE RULES AS YOU GO ALONG IS TOTALLY P-U-N-K. For me, knitting is a way to get out aggression and make something beautiful in the process, much like what music does for musicians." —KENDY P., MODESTO, CA

PUNK POET

This top came about one night when I was staring at a box of **safety pins.** It's knitted in three pieces—two fronts and a back. Knit it up, pin it together, add some black boots and a black skirt or shorts, and **you're stylin'.**

SIZES

To fit 34 (40)" bust

FINISHED MEASUREMENTS

28 (34)" chest unstretched; 34 (40)" stretched

MATERIALS

Yarn

Crystal Palace Punk (75% nylon / 25% polyester; 55 yards / 50 grams): 1 (2) balls #5094 melon meltdown (A), 1 (2) balls #5097 outrage orange (B), and 2 (3) balls #5099 posh pink (C)

Needles

One pair straight needles size US 13 (9 mm)
One pair straight needles size US 17 (12 mm)
Change needle size if necessary to obtain correct gauge.

Notions

2" long safety pins (at least 36); tapestry needle; elastic thread

GAUGE

8 sts and 10 rows = 4" (10 cm) in Stockinette stitch (St st) using smaller needles

2X2 RIB

(multiple of 4 sts; 1-row repeat)
All Rows: *K2, p2; repeat from * to end.

SLEEVELESS TOP

BOTTOM FRONT

Using larger needles and A, CO 28 (34) sts. (RS) Change to smaller needles. Begin St st. Work even for 4 rows. (RS) K2tog, knit to end—27 (33) sts remain. Purl 1 row. Repeat last two rows 15 (17) times—12 (16) sts remain. BO all sts loosely.

TOP FRONT

Using larger needles and B, CO 1 st.
Row 1: Knit.
Rows 2 and 4: Purl.
Row 3: K1-f/b—2 sts.
Row 5: Knit to last st, k1-f/b—3 sts.
Row 6: Purl.
Repeat Rows 5 and 6 13 (15) times—16 (18) sts.
(RS) Knit to end, using Cable CO method (see page 135), CO 12 (16) sts—28 (34) sts.

Work even until piece measures approximately 15 (16)" from the beginning, measuring along the long edge, including the gap between Bottom Front and Top Front. *Note: Be sure to allow enough of a gap to accommodate the length of the safety pins you will use.*

SHAPE ARMHOLE

BO 2 sts at beginning of next 2 rows, then 1 (2) sts at beginning of next 2 rows—22 (26) sts remain. Work even until armhole measures 7 (8)", ending with a WS row.

THIS PIECE IS FUN! Try different types of pins to hold the front together, or use contrasting yarns or leather laces. Experiment!

SHAPE SHOULDERS

BO 3 sts at beginning of next 2 rows, then 2 sts at beginning of next 2 rows—12 (16) sts remain.

SHAPE NECK

Change to 2x2 Rib. Work even until ribbing measures 9". BO all sts loosely in pattern. *Note: Be sure it will fit over the wearer's head before breaking yarn.*

JOIN FRONT PIECES

Join Top and Bottom together along the diagonal (shaping) edges with safety pins, matching each BO stitch of the Bottom piece to the adjacent CO stitch of the Top piece.

BACK

Using larger needles and C, CO 28 (34) sts. Change to smaller needles. Begin St st. Work even until piece measures same as for Front to armhole shaping, including gap and safety pins. Complete as for Top Front.

FINISHING

Sew shoulder, neck, and side seams. Using tapestry needle, thread elastic through BO edge of neck to reinforce elasticity of ribbing. Weave in all loose ends.

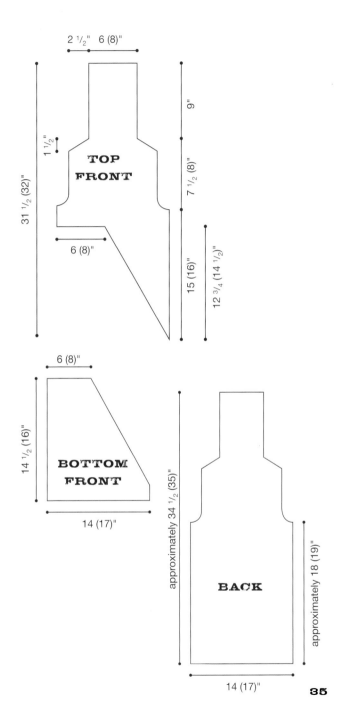

RATING/NIGHTCLUB

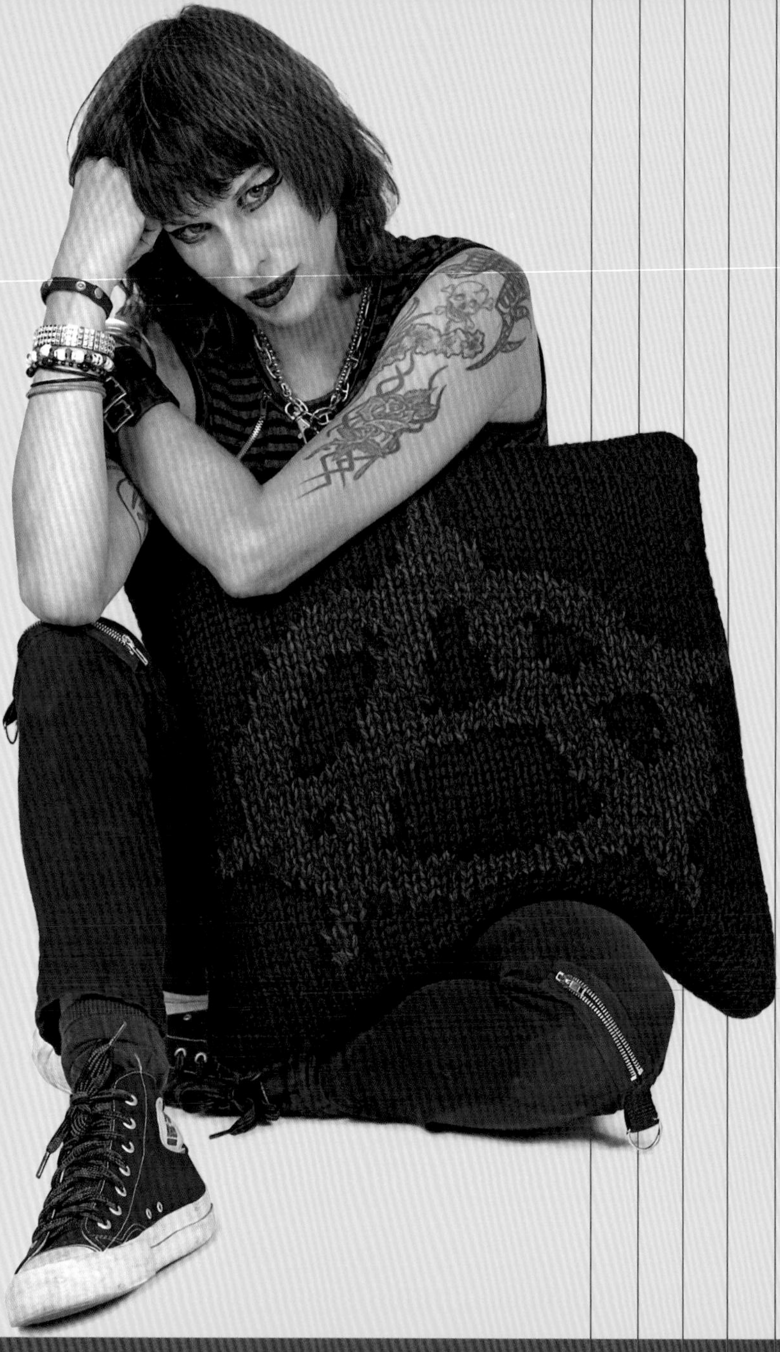

ANARCHY PILLOW

Who knew anarchy could be cuddly? What better way to get your point of view across than to kill them with kindness? This pillow was created for the New Millennium revolutionary.

Sleep with it.

Punch it with your rebellious anger.

Whisper your secret plans for **world peace through your knitting revolution.**

It's all about anarchy, baby. Now, go rule the universe with your new pillow.

FINISHED MEASUREMENTS
20" wide x 21" high

MATERIALS
Yarn
Rowan Yarns Big Wool (100% merino wool; 87 yards / 100 grams): 3 balls each #008 black (A), #028 bohemian (B)

Needles
One pair straight needles size US 15 (10 mm)
Change needle size if necessary to obtain correct gauge.

Notions
Yarn bobbins (optional); 20" square black pillow

GAUGE
10 sts and 12 rows = 4" (10 cm) in Stockinette st (St st)

NOTE
If a black pillow is not available, cover a white pillow form with black pillowcase or fabric to prevent the white surface from showing through the knitted cover.

PILLOW

FRONT
Using A, CO 50 sts; begin St st.
Work even for 10 rows.
Work Anarchy Motif: (RS) Continuing in St st, using Intarsia Colorwork Method (see page 135), begin Chart. Work 43 rows of Chart.
(WS) Using A, work even in St st for 10 rows. BO all sts.

BACK
Work as for Front, reversing colors.

FINISHING
Weave in ends. Block pieces to measurements.
Pin Front and Back together with WS's facing, so CO edge of Front lines up with BO edge of Back. RS facing, beginning in center of Front BO edge, using color of your choice, sew along edge to corner, then sew three full sides, making seams as invisible as possible. Insert pillow and sew remaining edge closed.

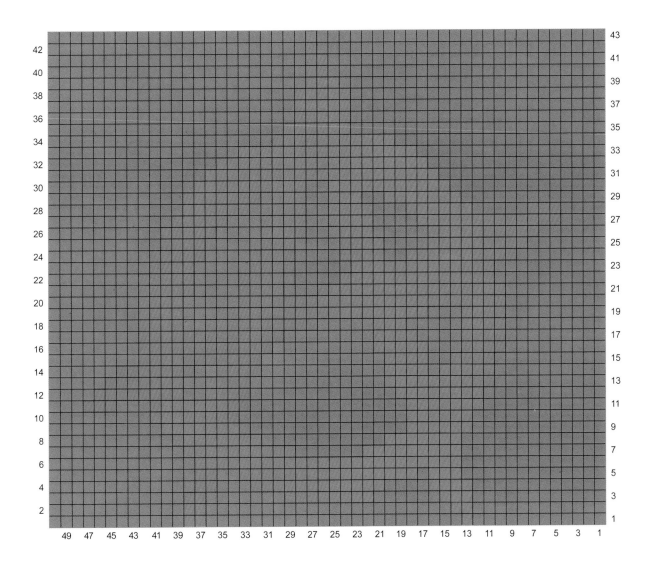

KEY

☐ St st—knit on RS, purl on WS

▧ A ▨ B

Note: reverse colors for Back.

RATING/THEATER • DESIGN/CATHERYN CLARKE

BILLION DOLLAR HAT

This felted hat's style impact varies depending on the wearer and the color of yarn used. Go with basic black and you're No More Mr. Nice Guy. Stick with the teal blue I chose and you're Billion Dollar Baby. **Either choice is ready to rock.** And let's face it, it's fun to be the conversation stopper when you walk into a room!

INSPIRATION: ALICE COOPER
Alice changed the face of rock 'n' roll forever with his blending of raw rock and theatrics. I had the extreme pleasure of touring with Mr. Cooper in 2002 and let me just say, he is one helluva performer and a very nice guy.

SIZES

One size

To fit average Adult

FINISHED MEASUREMENTS

32 1/4" circumference at brim, before felting; 21 1/4" after felting

11 3/4" height, before felting; 6 1/2" after felting

MATERIALS

Yarn

Brown Sheep Lamb's Pride Bulky (85% wool / 15% mohair; 125 yards / 100 grams): 2 skeins #M47 Tahiti teal

Needles

One set of four double-pointed needles (dpn) size US 10 (6mm)

One 29" (74 cm) circular needle (circ) size US 10 (6 mm)

Change needle size if necessary to obtain correct gauge.

Notions

Stitch markers

GAUGE

15 sts and 17 rows = 4" (10 cm) in Stockinette stitch (St st) before felting

I didn't have a professional hat shaper so **I STUFFED THE HAT WITH TOWELS** for each drying process!

FELTING IS FUN and has amazing results. Remember, it's best with a top-loading washing machine so you can stop it when necessary and the water won't spill out.

THE BILLION DOLLAR HAT IS EASY TO DECORATE! Use satin ribbons, peacock feathers, leather braid, chains, beaded necklaces, or anything else that suits your Alice personality!

HAT

CROWN

Note: Change to circ needle when necessary for number of sts.

Using dpn, CO 6 sts. Distribute sts evenly among 3 needles. Join for working in the rnd, being careful not to twist sts; place marker (pm) for beginning of rnd.

Rnds 1, 3, 5, 7, 9, 11, 13, 15, 17, 19, and 21: Knit.

Rnds 2 and 4: *K1, m1; repeat from * around—24 sts after Rnd 4.

Rnds 6 and 8: *K2, m1; repeat from * around—54 sts after Rnd 8.

Rnd 10: *K6, m1; repeat from * around—63 sts.

Rnd 12: *K7, m1; repeat from * around—72 sts.

Rnd 14: *K9, m1; repeat from * around—80 sts.

Rnd 16: *K10, m1; repeat from * around—88 sts.

Rnd 18: *K8, m1; repeat from * around—99 sts.

Rnd 20: *K9, m1; repeat from * around—110 sts.

Rnd 22: *K10, m1; repeat from * around—121 sts.

Rnd 23: Knit.

SHAPE HAT

Rnd 24 (turning rnd): Purl.

Rnd 25: *K9, k2tog; repeat from * around—110 sts remain.

Rnds 26–40: Knit.

Rnd 41: *K9, k2tog; repeat from * around—100 sts remain.

Rnds 42–51: Knit.

Rnd 52: *K8, k2tog; repeat from * around—90 sts remain.

Rnds 53–67: Knit.

Rnd 68: *K7, k2tog; repeat from * around—80 sts remain.

Rnds 69–73: Knit. Piece should measure 10" from Crown.

BRIM

Rnd 74 (turning rnd): Purl.

Rnd 75: *K5, m1; repeat from * around—96 sts.

Rnds 76–77: Knit.

Rnd 78: *K8, m1; repeat from * around—108 sts.

Rnds 79–80: Knit.

Rnd 81: *K9, m1; repeat from * around—120 sts.

Rnds 82–84: Knit.

Rnd 85: *K6, m1; repeat from * around—140 sts.

Rnds 86–88: Knit.

Rnd 89: *K7, m1; repeat from * around—160 sts.

Rnds 90–93: Knit.

Rnd 94: *K8, m1; repeat from * around—180 sts.

Work even in St st until Brim measures 4 1/2" from turning rnd.

BO all sts loosely.

FINISHING

Weave in all loose ends. Place completed Hat in a washing machine partially filled with hot water and a very small amount of detergent. Let it agitate for an entire cycle, checking every 10 minutes or so, and stopping when Hat reaches desired dimensions. Depending on the yarn used, this may take more than one cycle. (I washed mine three times.)

When felting is complete, rinse Hat in cold water and spin out excess water using the machine's spin cycle. Stuff hat with towels to hold shape until dry.

KOZMIK KAMI

If you hate to sew knitted pieces together, then the Kozmik Kami is the project to make because **there's no sewing involved**—it just laces up at the sides! But watch out when you wear it, because it will **turn heads wherever you go!**

INSPIRATION: JANIS JOPLIN
Her wild, sensual style and instantly recognizable whiskey voice reign supreme in the world of rockin' blues.

SIZES

To fit up to 36 (42)" bust

FINISHED MEASUREMENTS

21 $1/2$ (25)" chest (before unraveling dropped sts)

MATERIALS

Yarn

Debbie Bliss Cashmerino Aran (55% merino wool / 33% microfiber / 12% cashmere; 98 yards / 50 grams): 2 (3) balls #300 black (A)
Lana Grossa Viale (100% microfiber; 126 yards / 50 grams): 2 (3) balls #15 hot pink (B)
Rowan R2 Rag (100% cotton; 27 yards / 50 grams); 1 ball #01 black for Lacing (*Note: You may substitute any $1/2$"-wide ribbon yarn*)

Needles

One pair straight needles size US 10 $1/2$ (6.5 mm)
Change needle size if necessary to obtain correct gauge.

Notions

Stitch markers

GAUGE

18 sts and 20 rows = 4" (10 cm) in 2x2 Rib using one strand each of A and B held together

2X2 RIB

(multiple of 4 sts; 1-row repeat)
All Rows: *K2, p2; repeat from * across.

TANK

BACK

Note: Unravel all dropped sts down to CO edge.
With one strand each of A and B held together, CO 48 (56) sts. Begin 2x2 Rib. Work even until piece measures 10 (11)" from the beginning, ending with a WS row.
Next row (RS): BO 1 (3) sts, drop next st, BO in pattern to last 3 (5) sts, drop next st, BO last 2 (4) sts.

RIGHT FRONT

With one strand each of A and B held together, CO 24 (28) sts; begin 2x2 Rib. Work even until piece measures 10 (11)" from the beginning, ending with a WS row.

SHAPE NECK AND ARMHOLE

Dec Row (RS): Continuing in pattern as established, BO 1 (3) sts, drop next st, BO next 2 sts, work to end—20 (22) sts remain. Work even for 1 row.
(RS) BO 2 sts, work to end—18 (20) sts remain.
(WS) Repeat Dec Row—14 sts remain.
(RS) BO 4 sts at beginning of next 2 rows—6 sts remain.

STRAPS

Change to St st. Work even for 4 rows.
(RS) K2tog, k2, k2tog—4 sts remain. Purl 1 row.

The straps are worked in Stockinette stitch, **WHICH GIVES THEM A LITTLE ROLL.** If you prefer them without the roll, work them in Garter stitch (knit every row) instead.

The first time you drop a stitch in this piece, don't panic! You're supposed to do that. You may even have to help the ladder all the way down. Enjoy. Most patterns will tell you how to rescue a dropped stitch. With *Punk Knits*...**WE WANT DROPPED STITCHES!**

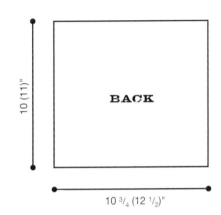

BACK

10 (11)"

10 ³/₄ (12 ½)"

Work even until Strap measures 11 (12)" from the beginning, ending with a WS row.
Next row (RS): K1, m1, k2, m1, k1—6 sts.
Work even for 5 rows. BO all sts loosely.

LEFT FRONT
Work as for Right Front, reversing all shaping.

FINISHING
Weave in all loose ends.
Place markers 2 ½ (3 ¼)" in from each armhole edge along BO edge of Back. Sew Straps to Back, centered on markers.

LACING
Cut ribbon yarn into three equal lengths. Using one piece, beginning at armhole and working down to waist, thread ribbon through holes created by dropped sts. Repeat for other side. With remaining length of ribbon, lace Fronts together from CO edge to neckline. Tighten ribbon as necessary to make Camisole fit comfortably. Trim excess ribbon.

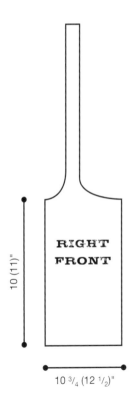

RIGHT FRONT

10 (11)"

10 ³/₄ (12 ½)"

RATING/ARENA

WOODSTOCK WAISTCOAT

This vest reflects a **Woodstockian aesthetic** with its natural colors and hip bohemian vibe. The stitchwork is based on an old lace pattern that repeats in a cool way and gives it a deconstructed look. Embellished with fur all around, it wears well on both guys and gals.

INSPIRATION: WOODSTOCK 1969

The most memorable rock festival of all time was undoubtedly Woodstock, and the most iconic moment in rock history was when Jimi Hendrix stepped on the stage as the final headliner of the three-day extravaganza. He blazed a trail where no musician had gone before and held the emotions of a nation in his guitar.

SIZES
Small (Medium, Large, X-Large)

FINISHED MEASUREMENTS
33 (37 1/2, 42 1/4, 47)" chest
16 1/2 (18 1/2, 21 1/2, 23 1/4)" back width

MATERIALS
Yarn
Manos del Uruguay Solid (100% wool; 138 yards / 100 grams): 2 (3, 3, 4) hanks #G coffee (A)
Crystal Palace Yarns Whisper (100% microfiber; 97 yards / 50 grams): 2 (3, 3, 4) balls #2841 cream (B)

Needles
One pair straight needles size US 10 1/2 (6.5 mm)
One 29" (74 cm) or 40" (102 cm) circular (circ) needle size US 13 (9 mm)
Change needle size if necessary to obtain correct gauge.

Notions
Stitch marker; row marker

GAUGE
10 sts and 12 rows = 4" (10 cm) in Broken Openwork Pattern using smaller needles and A

BROKEN OPENWORK PATTERN
(multiple of 6 sts + 1; 4-row repeat)
Row 1 (RS): *K2, yo, k1, [yo2, k1] twice, yo, k1; rep from * to last st, k1—13 sts.
Row 2: Knit, dropping yo's—7 sts remain.
Row 3: K1, yo2, k1, yo, k1, *k2, yo, k1, [yo2, k1] twice, yo, k1; rep from * to last 4 sts, k2, yo, k1, yo2, k1—25 sts.
Row 4: Rep Row 2—7 sts remain.
Repeat Rows 1–4 for Broken Openwork Pattern.

NOTES
Vest Fronts are narrower than Back and are designed to hang open. Choose size based on Back width.

Because this st pattern is reversible, you work the right and left Fronts exactly the same and then turn the left Front over, so that what was originally the WS becomes the RS.

Ladders are created by dropping yarnovers throughout, without knitting them.

When working increases and decreases, work extra stitches in Garter St until there are sufficient stitches to work a full repeat of Broken Openwork pattern.

Yo2: Wrap yarn around right-hand needle twice.

This piece uses a pattern I call Broken Openwork. Don't worry if you don't follow the pattern exactly—if you do a single yarnover (yo) instead of a double yarnover (yo2), that's fine. If you do a yo2 instead of a single yarnover, that's fine, too. As long as you mix it up and add in a few knit stitches, it will look wild. **ANY PATTERN IT CREATES WILL BE GREAT!** Knit with attitude!

VEST

BACK

Using smaller needles and A, CO 37 (43, 49, 55) sts. Begin Garter st (knit every row). Work even for 2 rows. Change to Broken Openwork Pattern. Work even until piece measures 8 (9, 10, 11)" from the beginning, ending with a WS row.

SHAPE BACK

(RS) Increase 1 st each side every 4 rows twice, working increased sts in Garter st—41 (47, 53, 59) sts. Work even until piece measures 10 (11, 13, 15)" from the beginning, ending with a WS row.

SHAPE ARMHOLE

(RS) BO 2 sts at beginning of next 4 rows, then decrease 1 st each side every other row 4 (4, 5, 6) times—25 (31, 35, 39) sts remain. Work even until piece measures 18 (19 1/2, 22, 24 1/2)" from the beginning, ending with a WS row.

SHAPE NECK

(RS) Work 10 (12, 14, 15) sts in pattern as established, join a second ball of yarn and BO center 5 (7, 7, 9) sts, work to end—10 (12, 14, 15) sts remain each side for shoulders.

(WS) Working both sides at the same time, BO 2 sts each neck edge 1 (2, 2, 2) times, then dec 1 st each side 1 (0, 0, 0) time—7 (8, 10, 11) sts remain each side for shoulders. Work even for one row.

SHAPE SHOULDERS

(RS) BO 3 (4, 5, 5) sts at beginning of next 2 rows, then 4 (4, 5, 6) sts at beginning of next 2 rows.

RIGHT AND LEFT FRONT
(BOTH ALIKE)

Using smaller needles and A, CO 4 sts.

SHAPE VEST POINTS

Row 1 (RS): Knit.
Row 2: K1, m1, k3—5 sts.
Row 3: K2, yo, k1, yo, k2—7 sts.
Row 4: K1, m1, knit to last st, dropping yo's, m1-r, k1—7 sts remain.
Row 5: K2, yo, k1, [yo2, k1] twice, yo, k2—13 sts.
Row 6: K1, m1, knit to end, dropping yo's—8 sts remain.
Row 7: K4, yo, k1, yo, k1, m1-r, k2—11 sts.
Row 8: Rep Row 4—11 sts.

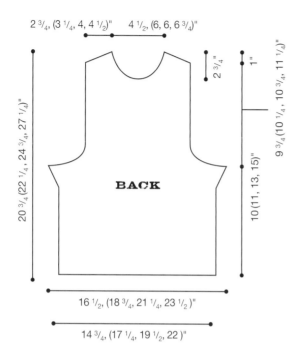

2 3/4, (3 1/4, 4, 4 1/2)"   4 1/2, (6, 6, 6 3/4)"

2 3/4"

1"

9 3/4 (10 1/4, 10 3/4, 11 1/4)"

BACK

20 3/4 (22 1/4, 24 3/4, 27 1/4)"

10 (11, 13, 15)"

16 1/2, (18 3/4, 21 1/4, 23 1/2)"

14 3/4, (17 1/4, 19 1/2, 22)"

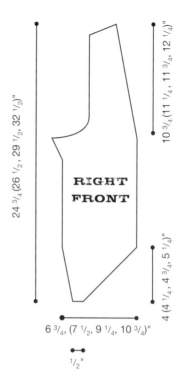

10 3/4 (11 1/4, 11 3/4, 12 1/4)"

RIGHT
FRONT

24 3/4 (26 1/2, 29 1/2, 32 1/2)"

4 (4 1/4, 4 3/4, 5 1/4)"

6 3/4, (7 1/2, 9 1/4, 10 3/4)"

1/2"

Row 9: K2, yo, k1, yo, k4, yo, k1, yo, k1, m1-r, k2—16 sts.

Row 10: Rep Row 6—13 sts remain.

Row 11: K2, yo, k3, yo, k2, [yo2, k1] twice, yo, k4—20 sts.

Row 12: Rep Row 4—15 sts remain.

Row 13: *K2, yo, k1, [yo2, k1] twice, yo, k1; repeat from * to last 3 sts, yo, k3—28 sts.

Row 14: Rep Row 6—16 sts remain.

Row 15: K2, yo2, k1, *yo, k3, yo, k1, [yo2, k1] twice; repeat from * to last st, k1—30 sts.

Row 16: Rep Row 6—17 sts remain.

Row 17: Work Row 1 of Broken Openwork Pattern. Continuing in Pattern as established, increase 1 st each side every row 0 (1, 3, 5) times, ending with a RS row—17 (19, 23, 27) sts. Place row marker for end of Vest point. Work even until piece measures 8 (9, 10, 11)" from marker for end of Vest point, ending with a WS row.

SHAPE FRONT

(RS) Increase 1 st at armhole edge every 4 rows twice—19 (21, 25, 29) sts. Work even until piece measures 10 (11, 13, 15)" from marker for end of Vest point, ending with a WS row.

SHAPE ARMHOLE AND NECK

(RS) BO 2 sts at armhole edge twice, then dec 1 st every other row 4 (4, 5, 6) times, and AT THE SAME TIME, decrease 1 st at neck edge every 6 rows 4 (5, 6, 8) times—7 (8, 10, 11) sts remain. Work even until piece, measured from marker for end of Vest point, measures same as for Back to shoulder. Shape shoulder as for Back.

FINISHING

Turn the left Front over so that what was originally the WS is now the RS. Sew shoulder and side seams.

FUR TRIM

RS facing, using larger circ needle and two strands of B held together, beginning at side seam, pick up and knit 4 sts for every 5 sts or rows around entire garment. Join for working in the rnd; place marker (pm) for beginning of rnd. Work in Garter st in-the-rnd (purl 1 rnd, k1 rnd) for 4 rnds. BO all sts loosely. Weave in all ends.

MOSH PIT CHOKER

Put on your punk clothes, add this choker, and you've got **classic**

style with a new twist.

Designed to be worn without pain or injuries in a mosh pit, this choker

is completely knit, right down to the studs!

INSPIRATION: SUZI QUATRO

Singer, bassist, radio personality, and actress, Quatro was the
queen of cool and led the glam rock invasion of the '70s.

FINISHED MEASUREMENTS

13 1/2" long x 1 1/2" wide (after blocking)

MATERIALS

Yarn

Sirdar Pure Cotton Double Knitting (100% cotton; 185 yards / 100 grams): 1 ball #0041 black (A)
Rowan Lurex Shimmer (80% viscose / 20% polyester; 100 yards / 25 grams): 1 ball #333 silver (B)

Needles

One set of four double-pointed needles (dpn) size US 3 (3.25 mm)
Change needle size if necessary to obtain correct gauge.

Notions

Stitch marker; tapestry needle; polyester fiberfill; jewelry clasp

GAUGE

24 sts and 32 rows = 4" (10 cm) in Stockinette stitch (St st) using A (before blocking)

Make two smaller versions for studded Wristies! Don't have a clasp that you like? **BE PUNK AND USE A SAFETY PIN!**

CHOKER

NECKBAND

Using A, CO 10 sts. Begin St st. Work even until piece measures 12" from the beginning. BO all sts.

STUDS (MAKE 5)

Using B, CO 10 sts and divide evenly among three dpn. Join for working in the rnd, being careful not to twist sts; place marker (pm) for beginning of rnd.
Rnds 1 and 2: Knit.
Rnd 3: *M1, k1; repeat from * around—20 sts. Re-distribute sts evenly among three needles.
Rnds 4 and 5: Knit.
Rnd 6: *K2tog; repeat from * around—10 sts remain. Remove marker.
Rnd 7: *K2tog; repeat from * until 4 sts remain.

BO all sts, leaving 7" tail. Using tapestry needle, thread tail around BO edge, reinforcing edge and closing gap. Fasten off. Draw remaining yarn through center of Stud to accentuate point. Trim end close to Stud.

FINISHING

Weave in all ends on neckband. Block piece to measurements.
Stuff Studs with polyester fiberfill.
Using tapestry needle and A, sew Studs to Neckband, spacing them evenly. Attach clasp.

WHAT KIND OF KNITTER ARE YOU?

LEAD SINGER

You like bold colors, novelty yarns, your own patterns, and garments that scream, "Hey, I'm here!" You will knit difficult items if they suit your personality.

BASS PLAYER

You tend toward a more muted palette, and you like to take other people's patterns and "improve" them with your own ideas. You prefer knitting items for others rather than for yourself.

LEAD GUITARIST

Ahhhh, you are the knitter who changes with the seasons. Sometimes you have to knit your own stuff and other times you like to knit along. You have a competitive streak that pushes you to higher levels in your knitting. Colors? Whatever mood you're in that day. You have a million projects on the go at once and can hardly remember which piece you should be working on when you walk in to your LYS.

DRUMMER

Your knitting is fun, fun, fun. If there is anything hard about the pattern, you've moved on to something else. You prefer garter stitch to anything with cables and you love to knit things up really fast. You give most of your knitting away.

RHYTHM GUITARIST

You're a knitter with a true eye for perfection. The garments you knit are unusually perfect and you pay great attention to detail. Colorwise, you are in the more quiet tones of the spectrum with an occasional bit of spice to add liveliness. Strengths? Complicated patterns and dpn's (double-pointed needles) are your best friends.

RATING/THEATER

DECON SWEATER

The Decon can be worn with jeans, over a T-shirt, or over just a black bra. Make it longer, make it with fewer holes, more holes…**it's very versatile.** It's up to you to put your stamp on it. I combined two yarns to create a fabric that I couldn't find in any single yarn. Experiment and **come up with your own fabulous yarn combos!** It's all about individuality!

INSPIRATION: KEITH RICHARDS

The one and only Keef. Having had the pleasure of meeting the legend himself at a Stones concert, I can say, with a shaky voice, that he is everything you want him to be and more. When I think of Keith Richards, I think of several things: his unbelievable legacy of songwriting and guitar playing, of course, plus his very hip, deconstructed, creative style.

SIZES

Small (Medium, Large)
Shown in size Small

FINISHED MEASUREMENTS

27 (31, 35)" chest, unstretched; 32 (37, 42)" chest, stretched
When choosing your size, consider how the fabric will be unstretched (at CO edge) and stretched (at chest) over the figure.

MATERIALS

Yarn
Adrienne Vittadini Nadia (50% alpaca / 50% wool; 71 yards / 50 grams): 5 (6, 7) hanks #808 smoke blue (A)
Karabella Yarns Aurora 8 (100% merino wool; 98 yards / 50 grams): 5 (5, 6) balls #14 denim (B)

Needles
One pair straight needles size US 17 (12 mm)
Change needle size if necessary to obtain correct gauge.

Notions
Stitch holder

GAUGE

8 sts and 10 rows = 4" (10 cm) in Stockinette stitch (St st) (unstretched) using one strand each of A and B held together

NOTES

Ladders are created by dropping yarnovers (yo's) throughout, without knitting them.

Yo2: Wrap yarn around right-hand needle twice without knitting.

Stitches are BO on RS rows and CO on WS rows to create holes in the fabric.

The pattern is written for a cropped top. Sweater may be adjusted for a longer length by inserting additional rows of Stockinette stitch where indicated. Additional yarn should be purchased for this option.

In this pattern I've included instructions for ALL of the holes to match the version of the sweater you see in the photo on page 58. However, it really is up to you where you place those holes! **SO DON'T WORRY IF YOU DEVIATE FROM THE PATTERN INSTRUCTIONS.** Place the "personality" where you want it.

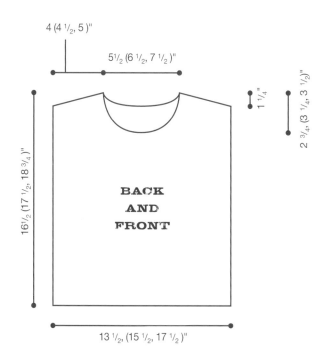

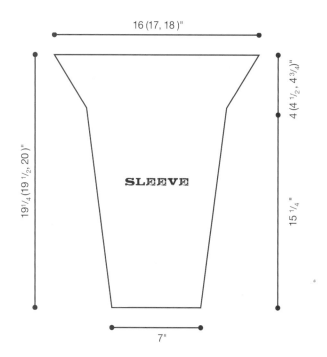

SWEATER

FRONT

With one strand each of A and B held together, CO 27 (31, 35) sts.

Row 1 (RS): Knit.

Row 2: K8 (10, 12), BO 5 sts, k8, BO 2 sts, knit to end—20 (24, 28) sts remain.

Row 3: K4 (6, 8), CO 2 sts, k8, CO 5 sts, k8 (10, 12)—27 (31, 35) sts.

Row 4: Knit.

Sizes M and L only: Continuing in St st, work even for 2 rows.

Note: For a longer sweater, additional rows of St st may be inserted here for all sizes. For every additional inch desired, add approximately two rows.

ESTABLISH PATTERN

Row 1: K9 (11, 13), [yo2, k1] 5 times, knit to end—37 (41, 45) sts.

Rows 2, 4, 14, 18, and 22: Purl, dropping all yo's.

Row 3: K20 (22, 24), [yo2, k1] 4 times, knit to end—35 (39, 43) sts.

Row 5: Knit.

Row 6: Purl.

Row 7: K3 (5, 7), [yo2, k1] 5 times, k3, BO 5 sts, knit to end—32 (36, 40) sts.

Row 8: P11 (13, 15), CO 5 sts, purl to end, dropping all yo's—27 (31, 35) sts remain.

Rows 9 and 10: Repeat Rows 5 and 6.

Row 11: K17 (19, 21), BO 6 sts, knit to end—21 (25, 29) sts remain.

Row 12: P4 (6, 8), CO 6 sts, purl to end—27 (31, 35) sts.

Row 13: K8 (10, 12), [yo2, k1] 4 times, knit to end—35 (39, 43) sts.

Row 15: K3 (5, 7), BO 4 sts, knit to end—23 (27, 31) sts remain.

Row 16: P20 (22, 24), CO 4 sts, purl to end—27 (31, 35) sts.

Row 17: K12 (14, 16), [yo2, k1] 5 times, knit to end—37 (41, 45) sts.

Row 19: K21 (23, 25), BO 2 sts, knit to end—25 (29, 33) sts remain.

Row 20: P4 (6, 8), CO 2 sts, purl to end—27 (31, 35) sts.

Row 21: K17 (19, 21), [yo2, k1] 4 times, knit to end—35 (39, 43) sts.

Row 23: K9 (11, 13), [yo2, k1] 5 times, k3, BO 3 sts, knit to end—34 (38, 42) sts.

Row 24: P4 (6, 8), CO 3 sts, purl to end, dropping all yo's—27 (31, 35) sts remain.

Rows 25 and 26: Repeat Rows 5 and 6.

Row 27: K3 (5, 7), BO 2 sts, k9, [yo2, k1] 3 times, knit to end—31 (35, 39) sts.

Row 28: P22 (24, 26), dropping all yo's, CO 2 sts, purl to end—27 (31, 35) sts.

Row 29: K21 (23, 25), BO 3 sts, knit to end—24 (28, 32) sts.

Row 30: P3 (5, 7), CO 3 sts, purl to end—27 (31, 35) sts.

Size L Only: Work even for 2 rows.

Note: For a longer sweater, additional rows of St st may be inserted here for all sizes. For every additional inch desired, add approximately two rows.

SHAPE NECK AND SHOULDER

(RS) K10 (12, 14), join a second ball each of A and B, BO center 7 sts, work to end—10 (12, 14) sts remain each side for shoulders. Working both sides at the same time, decrease 1 st each neck edge every row 2 (3, 4) times—8 (9, 10) sts remain each side for shoulders. BO 4 (4, 5) sts at beginning of next 2 rows, then 4 (5, 5) sts at beginning of next 2 rows.

BACK

Work as for Front to neck shaping, ending with a WS row—27 (31, 35) sts remain. Work even for 2 rows.

(RS) K10 (12, 14), [yo2, k1] 4 times, knit to end—35 (39, 43) sts.

(WS) Purl, dropping all yo's—27 (31, 35) sts remain.

Note: If additional rows were inserted on Front for a longer sweater, remember to make the same adjustments on Back.

SHAPE NECK AND SHOULDERS

(RS) Working both sides at the same time, BO 4 (4, 5) sts,

work 6 (8, 9) sts, join a second ball each of A and B, BO center 7 sts for neck, work to end. Working both sides at the same time, BO 4 (4, 5) sts at beginning of next row, then 4 (5, 5) sts at beginning of next 2 rows, and AT THE SAME TIME, BO 2 (3, 4) sts at each neck edge once.

SLEEVES (MAKE 2)

Using one strand each of A and B held together, CO 14 sts.
Row 1 (RS): Knit.
Row 2: Knit.
Row 3: K5, [yo2, k1] 4 times, knit to end—22 sts.
Row 4: Knit, dropping all yo's—14 sts remain.
Row 5: Knit.
Row 6: Purl.

SHAPE SLEEVE

Row 7: K1, m1, knit to last st, m1-r, k1—16 sts.
Row 8: Purl.
Row 9: K9, BO 2 sts, knit to end—14 sts remain.
Row 10: P5, CO 2 sts, purl to end—16 sts.
Row 11: K3, [yo2, k1] 3 times, knit to end—22 sts.
Row 12: Purl, dropping all yo's—16 sts remain.
Row 13: Knit.
Row 14: P1, m1-p, purl to last st, m1-p, p1—18 sts.
Rows 15 and 16: Repeat Rows 5 and 6.
Row 17: K10, [yo2, k1] 2 times, knit to end—22 sts.
Row 18: Repeat Row 12—18 sts remain.
Rows 19 and 20: Repeat Rows 5 and 6.
Row 21: Repeat Row 7—20 sts.
Row 22: Purl.
Row 23: K3, [yo2, k1] 3 times, knit to end—26 sts.
Row 24: Repeat Row 12—20 sts remain.
Row 25: K8, BO 3 sts, knit to end—17 sts remain.
Row 26: P9, CO 3 sts, purl to end—20 sts.
Row 27: Knit.

Row 28: Repeat Row 12—22 sts.
Rows 29 and 30: Repeat Rows 5 and 6.
Row 31: K16, [yo2, k1] 3 times, knit to end—28 sts.
Row 32: Repeat Row 12—22 sts.
Rows 33–38: Repeat Rows 5 and 6.

SHAPE CAP

Row 39: K1, m1, k7, BO 4 sts, knit to last st, m1, k1—20 sts remain.
Row 40: P11, CO 4 sts, purl to end—24 sts.
Row 41: K1, m1, k3, [yo2, k1] 3 times, knit to last st, m1, k1—32 sts.
Row 42: Repeat Row 12—26 sts remain.
Row 43: K1, m1, k13, [yo2, k1] 4 times, knit to last st, m1, k1—36 sts.
Row 44: Repeat Row 12—28 sts remain.
Row 45: Repeat Row 7—30 sts.
Row 46: Knit.
Row 47: Repeat Row 7—32 sts.

Sizes Medium and Large Only
Row 48: Knit.
Row 49: Repeat Row 7—34 sts.

Size Large Only
Row 50: Knit.
Row 51: Repeat Row 7—36 sts.

All Sizes
BO all sts loosely.

FINISHING

Sew shoulder seams. Measure down 8 (8 1/2, 9)" from shoulder seams on Front and Back; place markers. Sew Sleeves between markers. Sew side and Sleeve seams. Weave in all ends.

FAUX LOVE LOCKS

This one is for **non-knitters** who simply love yarn and want to make something cool for themselves! Make these faux dreadlocks in **outlandish colors** your hair would never produce naturally.

RATING/GARAGE • DESIGN/CATHERYN CLARKE

INSPIRATION: LENNY KRAVITZ
With or without his wildly swinging dreadlocks, Lenny is a legendary force of passion and creativity.

MATERIALS

Yarn

Colinette Point Five (100% wool; 54 yards /100 grams): 2 hanks #145 frangipani

Notions

Crochet hook size M–N / 13 (9 mm); 2 yards 1/2" elastic lace or mesh; bobby pins to match hair color; tape or heavy objects to use as anchors (books, bookends)

DREADLOCKS

Cut each hank of yarn into 60–75 strands, each 24" in length. Cut elastic lace in half to produce two 1–yard lengths.

Using tape or heavy objects like books or bookends as anchors, secure ends of lace to a table or other hard surface.

Beginning in the middle of the lace and working outward, attach each strand of yarn to the lace as you would attach Fringe (see page 135). Attach all the yarn from one hank to first piece of lace. Repeat with second hank for second piece of lace.

ATTACH DREADOCKS TO HAIR

Put your hair in two ponytails (or two buns, if your hair is long enough), one on either side of your head. Wrap each piece of lace around them as many times as you can, pinning in place with bobby pins to secure. Style Dreadlocks as desired.

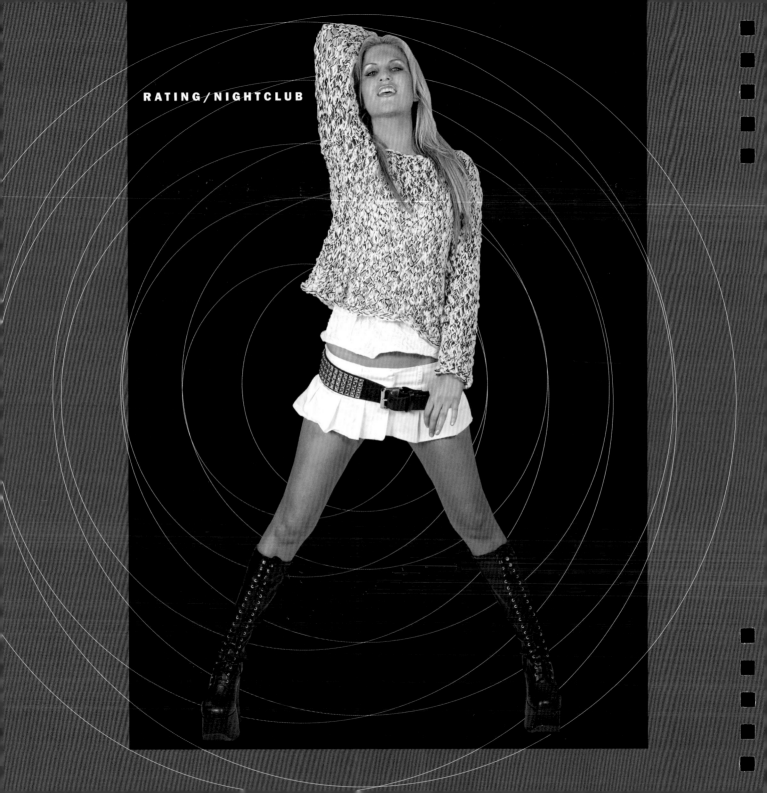

RATING/NIGHTCLUB

STARDUST SWEATER

Another **unisex piece**, you can make this for guys or chicks.

Make it longer. Add a different neckline. Wear it with jeans,

leathers, skirts—whatever suits your personal style.

The yarn I used is a premixed two-strand ribbon-wool combo that

comes in a variety of awesome colors. You can also **combine**

your own yarns for amazing results.

INSPIRATION: DAVID BOWIE

Blend a pop style with artistic sense, add some insanity, and mix
gently with an androgynous appeal . . . we love you, David.

SIZES
Small (Medium, Large)

FINISHED MEASUREMENTS
34 (37 1/2, 41)" chest

MATERIALS

Yarn
Berroco Vibe (64% wool / 36% nylon; 60 yards / 50 grams): 7 (8, 10) balls #4501 twelfth of never

Needles
One 26" (66 cm) circular (circ) needle size US 19 (15 mm)
One 26" (66 cm) circular needle size US 17 (12 mm)
Change needle size if necessary to obtain correct gauge.

GAUGE
9 sts and 12 rows = 4" (10 cm) in Eyelet Pattern using smaller needles

EYELET PATTERN
(multiple of 2 sts; 4-row repeat)
Row 1 (RS): *Yo, k2tog; repeat from * to end.
Row 2: Purl.
Row 3: *K2tog, yo; repeat from * to end.
Row 4: Purl.
Repeat Rows 1-4 for Eyelet Pattern.

NOTES
The Sweater is worked back and forth but on circular needles because circular needles accommodate the weight of the larger pieces more comfortably than straight needles.

The first and last stitches of each garment piece are selvage stitches (worked in St st throughout).

All shaping should be done inside the selvage sts.

SWEATER

BACK
Using larger needles, CO 38 (42, 46) sts.

ESTABLISH PATTERN
(RS) Change to smaller needles; k1 (selvage st, keep in St st), work in Eyelet Pattern across 36 (40, 44) sts, k1 (selvage st, keep in St st). Work even until piece measures 15 (16, 17)" from the beginning, ending with a WS row.

SHAPE ARMHOLE
(RS) Continuing in pattern and working selvage sts as established, BO 2 sts at beginning of next 2 rows, then 1 st at beginning of next 4 (4, 6) rows—30 (34, 36) sts remain. Work even until armhole measures 7 1/2 (8, 8 1/2)", ending with a WS row.

SHAPE SHOULDERS AND NECK
(RS) Work 9 (10, 11) sts, join a second ball of yarn and BO center 12 (14, 14) sts loosely, work to end. Decrease 1 st each neck edge once—8 (9, 10) sts remain each side for shoulders. BO all sts.

FRONT

Work as for Back until armhole measures 6 (6 1/2, 7)", ending with a WS row.

SHAPE NECK

(RS) Work 11 (12, 13) sts, join a second ball of yarn, BO center 8 (10, 10) sts loosely, work to end. Decrease 1 st each neck edge every row 3 times—8 (9, 10) sts remain each side for shoulders. Work even until armhole measures same as for Back to shoulder. BO all sts.

SLEEVE (MAKE 2)

Using larger needles, CO 18 sts. Begin Eyelet Pattern. Work even for 4 rows, ending with a WS row.

SHAPE SLEEVE

(RS) Increase 1 st each side this row, then every 9 (7, 5) rows 4 (5, 7) times, working increased sts in Eyelet Pattern as they become available—28 (30, 34) sts. Work even until Sleeve measures 17" from the beginning, ending with a WS row.

SHAPE CAP

(RS) BO 2 sts at beginning of next 2 rows, decrease 1 st each side every other row 3 (4, 5) times—18 (18, 20) sts remain. Work even for 1 row.

(RS) BO 2 sts at beginning of next 4 rows, then decrease 1 st each side once—8 (8, 10) sts remain. BO all sts loosely.

FINISHING

Block pieces to measurements. Sew shoulder seams. Set in Sleeves. Sew side and Sleeve seams. Weave in all ends.

3 1/2 (4, 4 1/2)" 6 1/4 (7, 7)"

2"

8 (8 1/2, 9)"

23 (24 1/2, 26)"

BACK AND FRONT

15 (16, 17)"

17 (18 3/4, 20 1/2)"

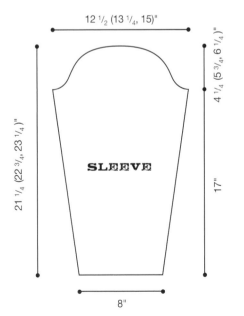

12 1/2 (13 1/4, 15)"

4 1/4 (5 3/4, 6 1/4)"

21 1/4 (22 3/4, 23 1/4)"

SLEEVE

17"

8"

RATING/NIGHTCLUB

THE ROCKER

Jeans and jean jackets have long been the staple of a musician's fashion diet. **Why not change it up** with some new handknitted sleeves? The style of your particular jacket body is going to determine exactly how you make and insert your sleeves, so use this pattern as a guide and then **improvise as necessary** for your particular situation.

INSPIRATION: LED ZEPPELIN

Jimmy, Robert, Bonzo, and John—the ultimate in rock. We mean Led Zeppelin. This jean jacket is named to honor their mastery of everything "heavy."

FINISHED MEASUREMENTS

8" armhole depth of jacket

9" cuff (knitted edge)

23" sleeve length (measured from shoulder to knitted edge of cuff)

MATERIALS

Yarn

GGH Esprit (100% nylon; 85 yards / 50 grams): 2 balls #12 slate blue

Needles

One pair straight needles size US 13 (9 mm)

Change needle size if necessary to obtain correct gauge.

Notions

Purchased jean jacket; sewing needle or sewing machine; thread to match yarn; scissors; seam ripper (optional); basting pins

GAUGE

8 sts and 13 rows = 4" (10 cm) in Stockinette stitch (St st)

Bear in mind, most jackets have a yoke! The jacket front and back are not symmetrical, so **EASE IN THE SLEEVE PROPORTIONALLY** around the armhole, eyeballing it as you go.

NOTES

Because jackets (and their wearers) come in infinite varieties, it is not possible to offer a pattern that will fit every style or size of jacket (the model is a size Small). The calculations required for *you* to create a pattern to match your jacket, however, are relatively simple.

Measure the circumference of your sleeve at the cuff and at the upper arm. For every additional 1/2" you need at the cuff, cast on 1 extra stitch. If you require a wider arm circumference, add an extra increase or two to the Sleeve shaping. (Each pair of increases adds one inch to Sleeve width.)

The Sleeve cap shaping is a bit trickier. Once you have removed the original jacket's sleeves, measure the armhole all the way around. That measurement will be the sum of the measurements in the Sleeve cap. In general, your sleeve width should be roughly twice the depth of your armhole. In our model, the knitted sleeve is 14" wide and 7" deep, easily fitting into the 8" deep jacket armhole (remember the knitted fabric stretches!).

Using the instructions here as a guideline, alter the Sleeve cap to match your jacket's armhole for best fit.

JACKET

PREPARE JACKET

With very sharp scissors, carefully remove cuffs from purchased jacket. Using a seam ripper or scissors, open seam at top of cuff. (This opening will receive the end of the knitted sleeve when you are ready to attach it.) Carefully cut off jacket sleeves at armhole edge. Measure the sleeve length before discarding, if you want your knitted Sleeve length to match.

SLEEVES (MAKE TWO)

CO 18 sts. Begin St st. Work even for 2 rows.

SHAPE SLEEVE

Next row (RS): Increase 1 st each side this row, then every 10 rows 4 times—28 sts. Work even until piece measures 16" or desired length from the beginning, ending with a WS row.

Note: Compare length of knitted Sleeve with original jacket sleeve to match fit, adding 1/2" for overlap when attaching to jacket cuff.

SHAPE CAP

(RS) BO 2 st at beginning of next 2 rows, decrease 1 st each side every other row 5 times, then every 4 rows twice, as follows: K1, ssk, knit to last 3 sts, k2tog, k1— 10 sts remain. BO all sts. Before breaking yarn, check Sleeve cap against jacket armhole for accurate fit. Remember your Sleeve cap will stretch!

FINISHING

Sew Sleeve seams, beginning at underarm and ending 2" from CO edge.

Set each Sleeve into armhole with jacket fabric on top of knitted Sleeve. Pin and baste around armhole edge before you commit! Sew by hand or machine, with matching thread.

Open edge of cuff where you previously removed stitching. Slide Sleeve about 1/2" into cuff, matching cuff placket with opening in Sleeve seam. The bottom of the Sleeve will remain partially open to mimic opening in jean jacket sleeve. Pin, baste, and machine or hand-sew Sleeve to cuff. Sew remainder of Sleeve seam if desired. Weave in all loose ends.

DESIGN/LISI GRINSTEIN • RATING/THEATER

MADLAD HAT

The Madlad Hat is a true classic. It just screams **vintage cool** as soon as you put it on. This hat can be made with or without the brim. If you bypass the brim, **you'll end up with a beret.** Either way, you'll look *très chic*.

INSPIRATION: JOHN LENNON

Well known for his extensive songwriting talents, John also exhibited quite the personality. When it came to his public image, he was the "madlad" in the Beatles with his mischievous replies and notorious antics. (*Madlad: Liverpudlian slang for an exuberant, high-spirited youth.*)

SIZES

To fit Small/Medium Adult

FINISHED MEASUREMENTS

21" circumference

MATERIALS

Yarn

Filtes King Kabir (50% wool / 50% acrylic; 70 yards / 50 grams): 2 balls #003 blue (A)
Sirdar Cossack Chunky (30% wool / 67% acrylic / 3% viscose; 147 yards / 100 grams): 1 ball #91 blue variegated (B)
Knit One, Crochet Two Douceur et Soie (65% baby mohair / 35% silk; 225 yards / 25 grams): 1 ball #8640 chambray (C)

Needles

One 16" (40 cm) circular (circ) needle size US 17 (12 mm)
Change needle size if necessary to obtain correct gauge.

Notions

Crochet hook size L/11 (8 mm); stitch markers; tapestry needle

GAUGE

8 sts and 12 rows = 4" (10 cm) in Stockinette stitch (St st) using one strand each of A, B, and C held together

NOTES

This pattern is for advanced knitters and requires basic crochet knowledge. The yarns I used are listed here, but it really is about intuition and trying out different combos to get the right fabric: thick enough but not too stiff. Have fun and imagine peace while knitting.

The Hat is worked throughout using one strand each of A, B, and C held together.

The Hat is turned WS out after completing the Crown, so that the WS becomes the RS. The Brim is then worked from the CO edge of the new RS.

Tightness or looseness of crochet finishing determines finished Hat size.

HAT

With one strand each of A, B, and C held together, CO 36 sts. Join for working in the rnd, being careful not to twist sts; place marker (pm) for beginning of rnd.
Rnds 1 and 2: *K3, p1; repeat from * around.

SHAPE HAT

Rnd 3: *K1, m1, k2, p1, k3, p1; repeat from * to last 4 sts, k1, m1, k2, p1—41 sts.
Rnd 4: *K4, p1, k3, p1; repeat from * to last 5 sts, k4, p1.
Rnd 5: *K4, p1, k1, m1, k2, p1; repeat from * to last 5 sts, k4, p1—45 sts.
Rnd 6: *K4, p1; repeat from * around.
Rnd 7: *K2, m1, k2, p1, k4, p1; repeat from * to last 5 sts, k2, m1, k2, p1—50 sts.
Rnd 8: *K5, p1, k4, p1; repeat from * to last 6 sts, k5, p1.
Rnd 9: *K5, p1, k2, m1, k2, p1; repeat from * to last 6 sts, k5, p1—54 sts.

Wear it like a Rasta hat. **OR WEAR IT TILTED A BIT TO THE SIDE.** Make it your own!

Rnd 10: *K5, p1; repeat from * around.
Rnd 11: *K3, m1, k2, p1, k5, p1; repeat from * to last 6 sts, k3, m1, k2, p1—59 sts.
Rnd 12: *K6, p1, k5, p1; repeat from * to last 7 sts, k6, p1.
Rnd 13: *K6, p1, k3, m1, k2, p1; repeat from * to last 6 sts, k5, p1—63 sts.
Rnds 14 and 15: *K6, p1; repeat from * around.

SHAPE CROWN

Rnd 16: *K2, k2tog, k2, p1; repeat from * around—54 sts remain.
Rnd 17: *K5, p1; repeat from * around.
Rnd 18: *K2, k2tog, k1, p1; repeat from * around—45 sts remain.
Rnd 19: *K4, p1; repeat from * around.
Rnd 20: *K1, k2tog, k1, p1; repeat from * around—36 sts remain.
Rnd 21: *K3, p1; repeat from * around.
Rnd 22: *K1, k2tog, p1; repeat from * around—27 sts remain.
Rnd 23: *K2, p1; repeat from * around.
Rnd 24: *K2tog, p1; repeat from * around—18 sts remain.

Break yarn, leaving 10" tail. Using tapestry needle, thread yarn through remaining sts twice, draw tight, and secure on RS. Turn WS out; what was previously the WS is now the RS. Weave in all ends.

BRIM

Note: The Brim of the Hat is worked across 13 CO sts, beginning and ending below a knit "rib."
Using crochet hook and one strand each of A, B, and C held together, secure yarn to CO edge of Hat at a knit "rib." Sc 13 sts around CO edge of Hat, ending at fourth purl stitch.

Row 1: Chain 1 and turn, sc in third sc, *sc in next 2 sc, 2 sc in next sc*; repeat from * to end of row.
Row 2: Repeat Row 1.
Row 3: Chain 1 and turn, sc in third sc and sc across row.
Row 4: Repeat Row 3.

Sc from end of Row 4 down side of Brim to CO edge. Continue sc around perimeter of Hat, adjusting the size of the Hat by the number and placement of sc sts. For a tighter fit, sc into every stitch; for a looser fit, sc into every other stitch.

When you have crocheted around to the beginning of the Brim, sc up the side of the Brim, ending at the beginning of Brim Row 4.

FINISHING

Break yarn and fasten off. Weave all ends into Brim securely.

SKULL KILT

Ahhhh, yes, the kilt! To be worn with confidence, black jeans or no jeans, black boots, and **definitely a ton of vibe!** Add your ripped fishnets, combat boots, and black lipstick, and you're ready for a Goth night on the town.

The skull sporran is attached with D–rings; the chain decorates all the way around. I added hanging beads to the bottom to weigh it down a bit. **Embellish this kilt with your own crafty flair** and make it completely unique.

I thought the guys I asked to try on this piece would object to it. I mean, it's a skirt, right? Boy, was I wrong! They each wanted one to keep as soon as possible. **So make no assumptions about a man in a kilt.** He can be full of surprises.

INSPIRATION: MARILYN MANSON

Theatrical goth musician, Manson keeps entertaining us while giving us slammin' rock sounds. Controversy is his middle name and we like it that way!

SIZES
Medium (Large)
Shown in size Medium

FINISHED MEASUREMENTS
KILT
30 (35 $1/2$)" waist, unstretched; 34 (40 $1/2$)" stretched
44 $1/2$ (51 $1/2$)" hip
18 (19)" length, including finished waistband
SPORRAN
Approximately 8" wide x 8 $1/2$" long

MATERIALS
Yarn
Crystal Palace Yarns Merino Frappe (80% merino / 20%
nylon; 140 yards / 50 grams): 8 (10) balls #006 black
(A), 1 ball #010 ivory (C)
Crystal Palace Yarns Raggedy (50% acrylic / 30% nylon
/ 20% wool; 56 yards / 50 grams): 7 (9) balls #2182
black (B)

Needles
One pair straight needles size US 15 (10 mm)
One pair straight needles size US 11 (8 mm)
One pair straight needles size US 6 (4 mm)
Change needle size if necessary to obtain correct gauge.

Notions
Stitch markers; one yard 1"-wide, non-rolling black elastic
for waistband; sewing needle and thread; needle-nose pliers; five 1" D-rings; four 1" rectangular rings; five $1/2$" O-
rings; assorted beads and chains to embellish the Sporran

GAUGE
9 sts and 10 rows = 4" (10 cm) in Kilt Pattern Stitch
using largest needles and one strand each of A and B
held together

KILT PATTERN STITCH
(multiple of 8 sts + 2; 2-row repeat)
Row 1 (RS): K1, *k7, p1; repeat from * to last st, k1.
Row 2: K4, *p1, k7*; repeat from * to last 6 sts, p1, k5.
Repeat Rows 1 and 2 for Kilt Pattern Stitch.

NOTES
The Skull Chart is worked in St st and surrounded on all sides by
a Garter st border to prevent the Sporran from curling. The Chart
is worked in two colors, using the Stranded (Fair Isle) Colorwork
Method (see page 135).

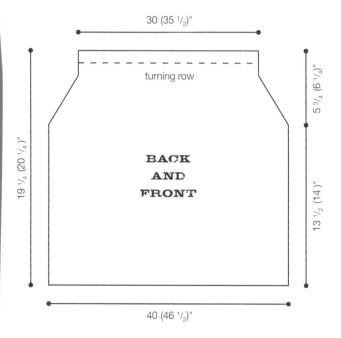

30 (35 $1/2$)"

turning row

5 $3/4$ (6 $1/4$)"

19 $1/4$ (20 $1/4$)"

BACK
AND
FRONT

13 $1/2$ (14)"

40 (46 $1/2$)"

**THIS PIECE HAS A DEFINITE
RHYTHM TO IT.** Familiarize yourself with the stitch
pattern and pretty soon it will fly off your needles.

Working with two yarns held together can be a little tricky. **TO
AVOID TANGLING THE YARNS,** keep each
ball in a separate zip-top bag. Don't worry about the Raggedy
yarn twisting around too much; it will still look cool.

KEY

■ A □ B

*Note: Chart is worked in St st—
knit on RS, purl on WS*

KILT

BACK AND FRONT (BOTH ALIKE)

Using largest needles and one strand each of A and B held together, CO 50 (58) sts. Begin Kilt Pattern Stitch. Work even until piece measures 13 1/2 (14)" from the beginning, ending with a WS row. Make it longer if it suits your taste!

SHAPE WAIST

Change to size US 11 needles, St st, and 1 strand of B.

Row 1 (RS): Knit.

Row 2 and all WS rows: K1, purl to last st, k1.

Row 3: K2tog, knit to last 2 sts, k2tog—48 (56) sts remain.

Row 5: Knit.

Row 7: Knit.

Row 8: Repeat Row 2.

Repeat Rows 3–8 once (twice)—46 (52) sts remain.

Size Medium Only: Repeat Rows 3–6 once—44 sts remain.

WAISTBAND

Row 1 (RS): K1, purl to last st, k1 (turning row).

Row 2: K1, purl to last st, k1.

Row 3: Knit.

Repeat Rows 2 and 3 once.

BO all sts loosely.

FINISHING

Sew Side seams.

Measure your waist. Cut length of elastic 2" shorter than waist measurement and sew ends together. Fold Waistband over elastic to WS at turning rnd. Sew BO edge to WS of Skirt, being careful not to let sts show on RS. Weave in all ends.

SPORRAN

Using smallest needles and A, CO 39 sts. Begin Garter St (knit every row). Work even for 4 rows, place marker (pm) after st #4 and #36 on last row.

ESTABLISH CHART

(RS) K4, work across 31 sts from Chart, k4. Work even until entire Chart is complete, working sts before and after Chart in Garter st.

Continuing in A, work in Garter st across all sts. Work even for 4 rows, removing markers on first row. BO all sts loosely.

FINISHING

Block piece if desired. Weave in all loose ends.

Add your favorite hanging beads to the bottom of the Sporran for a cool fringe effect. This also helps to weigh it down. I used sets of pre-strung beads 3/4" long, and attached each one directly to the CO edge of the Sporran using pliers and a jump ring.

Using needle-nose pliers, attach 4 rectangular rings evenly spaced across the top edge of the Sporran (see photo). You can attach these rings directly to the front of the Kilt, or do what I did: Attach 5 D-rings (2 in the Front and 3 in the Back) to the Kilt, one inch below the waistband. Join a small O-ring to each of the bigger rings. Thread one or more chains through each O-ring around the Kilt and through the rectangular rings on the Sporran. *Note: Do not attempt to mess with the rings until you've sewn in all those loose ends!*

SWINGIN' GAUNTLETS

These gauntlets, which are laced together through holes created from dropped stitches, are deliciously dressy and add an elegant flair to any outfit. I knitted them in Berroco Optik to create a **raggedy, wild look.** You can experiment with "cleaner" yarns, but the Optik pulls together the **deconstructed style with a flourish.** These knit up very fast and are verrrrry fun to wear!

INSPIRATION: MARIANNE FAITHFULL

A '60s celebrity superstar, then a heroin addict on the streets of New York, Marianne is back to health and performing better than ever, proof that she is one helluva lady.

FINISHED MEASUREMENTS

9 1/2" circumference below elbow, unstretched
15 " long palm to elbow

MATERIALS

Yarn

Berroco Optik (48% cotton / 21% acrylic / 20% mohair / 8% metallic / 3% polyester; 87 yards / 50 grams): 1 ball #4918 Seine

Needles

One pair straight needles size US 6 (4 mm)
Change needle size if necessary to obtain correct gauge.

Notions

Crochet hook size US G/6 (4mm) (optional); 7 yards 1/2" wide Hanah Silk Ribbon fallen leaves

GAUGE

20 sts and 16 rows = 4" (10 cm) in 2x2 Rib (before dropping sts)

2X2 RIB

(multiple of 4 sts; 1-row repeat)
All Rows: *K2, p2; repeat from * to end.

This yarn can be tricky. Feel free to knit these with bigger needles to make it easier. **FOR THE DROPPED STITCHES, BE PATIENT.** Use two hands and work the stitches all the way down. It's worth it to wear these out on the town and mention that you knit them in an evening!

NOTES

Gauntlets are worked from just below the elbow to the palm of the hand.

Before dropping sts to create "ladders" at the very end, these will look extremely skinny and impossible to wear. Have no fear! They'll fit.

The Thumbhole is created by working with separate balls of yarn on either side of a vertical "keyhole." To save time later, wind off a second, small ball from the original ball before beginning.

"I love the raw edginess of punk style. **THE LOOK IS UNCONVENTIONAL, UNFINISHED, AND COMPLETELY ORIGINAL.** I believe everyone has a bit of punk hidden inside of them somewhere. " —JESSICA M., SWAMPSCOTT, MA

GAUNTLETS

CO 20 sts; begin 2x2 Rib. Work even until piece measures 11" from the beginning.

Establish Thumbhole: (RS) Work in pattern as established for 8 sts; join a second ball of yarn and work to end.

Working both sides of Thumbhole at same time, work even until Thumbhole opening measures approximately 2", ending with a WS row; break second ball of yarn.

(RS) Work across all sts. Continue until piece measures 15" from the beginning, ending with a WS row.

Dropped St BO: (RS) K1, drop 1 st off needle, BO 16 sts (beginning with first st knit), drop 1 st, BO remaining sts. Unravel dropped sts down to the CO row.

FINISHING

Weave in all ends.

THUMBHOLE EDGING (OPTIONAL)

Using crochet hook, work 1 row single crochet around Thumbhole for a finished look.

Cut ribbon into 2 equal lengths. Using one piece, beginning at BO edge of Gauntlet, thread ribbon through holes created by dropped sts. Weave in and out every 2 to 3 sts. Tighten ribbon as necessary to make Gauntlet fit comfortably. Tie ribbon ends at top, just below elbow.

Make a second Gauntlet to match the first.

MOTHER'S DM WARMERS

These DM warmers were **made to be worn with Doc Martens** (hence the name) but of course, you can wear them with any shoes or boots you like. Why three yarns, you might ask? Good question! I wanted to **get that furry look** where the length and thickness of all the furs were different. The only way to get it seemed to be triple-stranding.

INSPIRATION: FRANK ZAPPA

The mere name instills fear and awe in almost any musician. Mr. Zappa created some of the most amazing and unusual music to ever descend upon the universe as we know it. He was the ultimate punk who did his own thing and never considered conformity an option.

FINISHED MEASUREMENTS

8" circumference, unstretched; 17" stretched
16" length

MATERIALS

Yarn

S. R. Kertzer Baby Monkey (100% nylon; 55 yards /
50 grams): 2 balls #8 gray (A)
Idena Happy (100% polyester; 99 yards / 50 grams):
1 ball #990 jet black (B)
Lana Grossa Pep Print (80% microfiber / 20% polyam-
ide; 120 yards / 50 grams): 1 ball #315 taupe (C)

Needles

One 16" (40 cm) circular (circ) needle size US 15
(10 mm)
Change needle size if necessary to obtain correct
gauge.

Notions

Stitch marker

GAUGE

9 sts and 24 rows = 4" (10 cm) in Stockinette stitch
(St st) using one strand each of A, B, and C held
together

2X2 RIB

(multiple of 4 sts; 1-rnd repeat)
All Rnds: *K2, p2; repeat from * around.

NOTE

Be sure to BO all sts loosely so Warmers will fit over
DMs.

THESE ARE KNIT FROM THE
BOTTOM UP. They will look quite long when you are
finished but acquire that super scrunched-up style when you
put 'em on!

WARMERS

Using one strand each of A, B, and C held together, CO 24
sts. Join for working in the rnd, being careful not to twist
sts; place marker (pm) for beginning of rnd. Begin 2x2
Rib. Work even for 4 rnds.

SHAPE LEG

Change to St st.
Dec Rnd 1: *K4, k2tog; repeat from * around—20 sts
remain. Work even until piece measures 3 1/2" from the
beginning.
Dec Rnd 2: [K2tog, k8] twice—18 sts remain. Work even
until piece measures 14" from the beginning.
Dec Rnd 3: [K2tog, k7] twice—16 sts remain.
Change to 2x2 Rib. Work even for 6 rnds. BO all sts
loosely in pattern.

FINISHING

Weave in all loose ends.

Make a second Warmer to match the first.

THUNDERBIRD SCARF

Wear this scarf with a half Windsor knot and go for the mod look! As for knitting it up fast? **This is super speedy!** Featuring a classic drop-stitch pattern, this scarf looks great knitted in variegated and thick-thin novelty yarns.

INSPIRATION: RONNIE WOOD

Ronnie Wood, a superb artist and amazing guitarist, became the "new guy" in the Rolling Stones. The name of his first band, The Thunderbirds, also recalls a very cool bass and an ultra-cool muscle car.

FINISHED MEASUREMENTS

5 1/4" wide x 66" long

MATERIALS

Yarn

Rio De la Plata Wool Multi (100% wool; 140 yards / 99 grams): 1 ball #M67 black, ethereal blue, fuschia (A) Karabella Yarns Lace Mohair (61% super kid mohair / 31% polyester / 8% wool; 540 yards / 50 grams): 1 ball #250 black (B)

Needles

One pair straight needles size US 15 (10 mm) Change needle size if necessary to obtain correct gauge.

GAUGE

10 sts and 8 rows = 4" (10 cm) in Openwork Pattern

OPENWORK PATTERN

(multiple of 2 sts + 1; 4-row repeat)
Row 1 (RS): Knit.
Row 2: Knit.
Row 3: K1, *yo, k1; repeat from * across.
Row 4: Knit, dropping yo's.
Repeat Rows 1–4 for Openwork Pattern.

This scarf can be knit with a single strand of yarn or with two strands of yarn held together **TO GIVE IT EXTRA TEXTURE.**

SCARF

Using one strand each of A and B held together, CO 13 sts. Begin Openwork Pattern. Work even until piece measures 66" or desired length from the beginning. BO all sts.

FINISHING

Weave in all loose ends.

RATING / GARAGE

BOMBSHELL SKIRT

This skirt is very mini. You can, of course, make it longer to suit your taste. Or...make it shorter to suit your wild side. The dropped stitches give it a nice effect and automatically make it wider at the bottom. **Want more flare? Add more drops!** To be worn with attitude and style.

INSPIRATION: BLONDIE
Especially Debbie Harry, the band's incomparably iconic peroxide-blonde lead singer.

SIZES
One size fits most

FINISHED MEASUREMENTS
25 (28, 31, 34 1/2)" waist, unstretched; 28 (31 1/2, 35, 39)" stretched
29 1/2 (33, 36, 39)" hip, unstretched; 33 (37, 40 1/2, 44)" stretched
12 (13, 15, 17)" length

MATERIALS
Yarn
Berroco Plush (100% nylon; 90 yards / 50 grams): 2 (2, 3, 4) balls #1947 bubblegum (A)
Cascade Fixation (98.3% cotton / 1.7% elastic; 100 yards / 50 grams): 1 (2, 2, 3) balls #3077 pink lemonade (B)

Needles
One pair straight needles size US 11 (8 mm)
One pair straight needles size US 10 (6 mm)
Change needle size if necessary to obtain correct gauge.

Notions
One yard 1"-wide non-rolling elastic; sewing needle and thread

GAUGE
10 sts and 16 rows = 4" (10 cm) in Stockinette stitch (St st), using larger needles and one strand each of A and B held together.

NOTES
When choosing size, keep in mind that this fabric is very stretchy.

Skirt is worked flat in two pieces, from hem to waistband casing.

SKIRT

BACK AND FRONT (BOTH ALIKE)
Using larger needles and one strand each of A and B held together, CO 37 (41, 45, 49) sts. Knit 3 rows. Change to St st, beginning with a purl row, and work even until piece measures 4 (5, 6, 7)" from the beginning, ending with a RS row.

SHAPE SKIRT
Note: After dropping a stitch, unravel it all the way down to the cast-on edge.
Next row (WS): P11 (12, 13, 14), drop next st, purl to end—36 (40, 44, 48) sts remain. Continuing in St st, work even until piece measures 5 (6, 7, 8)" from the beginning, ending with a RS row.

Next row (WS): P24 (27, 32, 36), drop next st, purl to end—35 (39, 43, 47) sts remain. Continuing in St st, work even until piece measures 6 (7, 8, 9)" from the beginning, ending with a RS row.

Next row (WS): P5 (6, 6, 7), drop next st, purl to end—34 (38, 42, 46) sts remain. Continuing in St st, work even until piece measures 8 (9, 10, 11)" from the beginning, ending with a RS row.

I have included the exact stitches I dropped for this skirt in the pattern, but **YOU CAN DROP STITCHES WHEREVER YOU LIKE.** I chose these particular stitches to place the ladders mainly in the leg area.

Next row (WS): P30 (34, 37, 41), drop next st, purl to end—33 (37, 41, 45) sts remain.

Continuing in St st, work even until piece measures 11 (12, 14, 15)" from the beginning, ending with a WS row.

Dec Row (RS): Decrease 1 st each side—31 (35, 39, 43) sts remain.

Work even until piece measures 12 (13, 15, 17)" from the beginning, or to desired length to Waistband, ending with a WS row.

WAISTBAND

(RS) Purl 1 row (turning row). Change to smaller needles. Continuing in St st, work even for 5 rows. BO all sts loosely.

FINISHING

Sew side seams.
Measure your waist. Cut length of elastic 2" shorter than waist measurement and sew ends together. Fold Waistband over elastic to WS at turning row. Sew BO edge to WS of Skirt, being careful not to let sts show on RS.

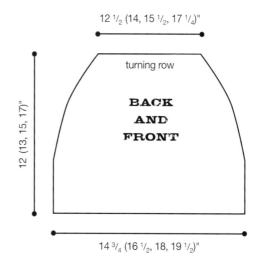

12 1/2 (14, 15 1/2, 17 1/4)"

turning row

BACK AND FRONT

12 (13, 15, 17)"

14 3/4 (16 1/2, 18, 19 1/2)"

RATING/NIGHTCLUB • DESIGN/CATHERYN CLARKE

BANSHEE OVER-THE-KNEE HI'S

Wear these **cool flared leggings** with boots for a tough look or match them up with heels for a dressy look. I chose to knit them in **sexy black,** but you can use any color yarn you fancy, of course.

FINISHED MEASUREMENTS

6 ¹/₂" circumference, unstretched; 16" stretched
24" length

MATERIALS

Yarn

Crystal Palace Yarns Choo-Choo (52% rayon / 30% polyester / 18% nylon; 92 yards / 50 grams): 3 balls #4654 black/red (A)
Cascade Yarns Fixation (98.3% cotton / 1.7% elastic; 100 yards / 50 grams): 1 ball #8990 black (B)

Needles

One pair straight needles size US 11 (8 mm)
One pair straight needles size US 10 (6 mm)
Change needle size if necessary to obtain correct gauge.

GAUGE

20 sts and 15 rows = 4" (10 cm) in 2x3 Rib using larger needles and A

2X3 RIB

(multiple of 5 sts; 2-row repeat)
Row 1 (RS): *K2, p3; repeat from * across.
Row 2: Knit the knit sts and purl the purl sts as they face you.
Repeat Row 2 for 2x3 Rib.

NOTES

These Knee Hi's extend from the instep to the knee, and are knit from the bottom up. Unlike traditional Knee Hi's, these are footless.

Ribbing at the knee holds the Knee Hi's in place. The yarn used contains elastic, which allows the cuff to stretch up to 16". Keep this in mind if substituting yarns.

Shaping is accomplished by dropping purl stitches between knit "ribs;" the 2x3 Rib becomes a 2x2 Rib in this manner.

Want more of a flare at the bottom? Cast on more stitches and drop them at even intervals. **VOILÀ: MORE FLARE.**

"Knitting is punk because it is immediate and visceral. There is not much room in knitting for over-analysis or neurosis—IT IS PURE SENSORY DELIGHT IN ITS MOST BASIC FORM. And the finished product can be as refined and palatable as a Blondie tune, or evoke the raw mayhem of the Dead Kennedys!" —HEATHER M., SUNNYVALE, CA

KNEE HI'S

Using A and larger needles, CO 40 sts. Begin 2x3 Rib. Work even until piece measures 4" from the beginning, ending with a WS row.

SHAPE LEG

Note: Unravel all dropped sts down to CO row.
Dec Row 1 (RS): K2, p1, drop st, p1, k2, [p3, k2] 3 times, p1, drop st, p1, k2, [p3, k2] twice, p3—38 sts remain.
Row 1: K3, [p2, k3] twice, p2, k2, [p2, k3] 3 times, p2, k2, p2.
Row 2: K2, p2, [k2, p3] 3 times, k2, p2, [k2, p3] 3 times.
Repeat Rows 1 and 2 until piece measures 5 1/2" from the beginning, ending with a WS row.

Dec Row 2 (RS): *K2, p2, k2, p1, drop st, p1, k2, p3, k2, p1, drop st, p1; repeat from * to end—34 sts remain.
Row 1: K2, p2, k3, p2, [k2, p2] 3 times, k3, p2, [k2, p2] twice.
Row 2: K2, [p2, k2] twice, p3, k2, [p2, k2] 3 times, p3, k2, p2.
Repeat last two rows until piece measures 7" from the beginning, ending with a WS row.

Dec Row 3 (RS): K2, [p2, k2] twice, p1, drop st, p1, k2, [p2, k2] 3 times, p1, drop st, p1, k2, p2—32 sts remain.
Next row (WS): *K2, p2; repeat from * across. Work even until piece measures 24" or desired length from the beginning. Cuff should fall just above wearer's knee.

CUFF

Change to smaller needles and one strand each of A and B held together. Work even until piece measures 26" from the beginning, ending with a WS row. BO all sts loosely in pattern, leaving a 36" tail.

FINISHING

Using tail, sew side seam. Weave in all loose ends.

Make a second Knee Hi to match the first.

RATING / ARENA

NEW YORK DOLLY

Wear it, be it, state it without apology. Yeah. This **jacket/vest/long cardigan,** embellished with dropped stitches, carries unstoppable energy! As with almost everything in *Punk Knits*, you can **change the length** and/or the placement of the dropped stitches **to suit your taste!**

INSPIRATION: THE NEW YORK DOLLS

In your face and full of bravado, they tore up the music business and spit it back out! Mixing up lipstick and smeared eyeliner with rock 'n' roll that became a classic look and sound, the New York Dolls left a legacy in both music and style.

SIZE
One Size

FINISHED MEASUREMENTS
35 ½" chest

MATERIALS

Yarn
Crystal Palace Yarns Iceland (100% wool; 109 yards / 100 grams): 8 balls #0008 cerise (A)
Crystal Palace Yarns Whisper (100% microfiber nylon; 97 yards / 50 grams): 4 balls #2843 ebony (B)

Needles
One 24" (60 cm) circular (circ) needle size US 10½ (6.5 mm)
One 29" (73 cm) circular needle size US 13 (9 mm)
One 16" (40 cm) circular needle size US 13 (9 mm) for Armhole Edging (optional)
Change needle size if necessary to obtain correct gauge.

Notions
Stitch markers; five 2" black buttons; five 1" black buttons for backing

GAUGE
14 sts and 20 rows = 4" (10 cm) in Stockinette stitch (St st) using A and smaller needle (before dropping sts)

NOTES
This piece is knit back and forth, but a circular needle is recommended because of the weight of the yarn.

Each dropped stitch adds approximately 3/4" to the width of the finished piece.

An openwork border is worked around all edges of the piece up to the armholes.

All shaping is worked to the inside of the border sts.

Yarnovers within the border are used as buttonholes in the finished piece.

When working the contrasting trim, I picked up 3 sts for every 4 on the horizontal edges, and 1 st for every 2 rows on the vertical edges. You may use the pick-up numbers given, or use whatever pick-up ratio gives you a pleasing edge.

I used **BIG BUTTONS** to make a statement with the New York Dolly. You can add a lot of details to this piece: **POCKETS, BUTTONS, OR CONTROLLED DROPPED STITCHES.**

VEST

BACK

Using smaller needle and A, CO 72 sts.

Row 1 (RS): K1, *k1, yo: repeat from * to last st, k1—142 sts.

Row 2: Knit, dropping all yo's—72 sts remain.

Rows 3 and 4: Repeat Rows 1 and 2 once.

ESTABLISH PATTERN

Row 5: K1, [k1, yo] twice, place marker (pm), knit to last 3 sts, pm, [yo, k1] twice, k1—76 sts.

Row 6: Purl, dropping all yo's.

Repeat Rows 5 and 6 until piece measures 6" from the beginning, ending with a WS row.

SHAPE BODY

Note: Unravel all dropped sts down to CO row.

(RS) K1, [k1, yo] twice, k15, drop next st, k34, drop next st, k15, [yo, k1] twice, k1—74 sts. Purl 1 row, dropping all yo's—70 sts remain. Work even until piece measures 9" from the beginning, ending with a WS row.

(RS) K1, [k1, yo] twice, k10, drop next st, k13, drop next st, k14, drop next st, k13, drop next st, k10, [yo, k1] twice, k1. Purl 1 row, dropping all yo's—66 sts remain. Work even until piece measures 12" from the beginning, ending with a WS row.

(RS) K1, [k1, yo] twice, k4, drop next st, k23, drop next st, k2, drop next st, k23, drop next st, k4, [yo, k1] twice, k1. Purl 1 row, dropping all yo's—62 sts remain. Work even until piece measures 24" from the beginning, ending with a WS row.

SHAPE ARMHOLE

Change to St st, omitting openwork border. BO 3 sts at beginning of next 2 rows, then decrease 1 st each side every other row 4 times—48 sts remain. Work even until armhole measures 8 1/2", ending with a WS row.

SHAPE SHOULDERS AND NECK

(RS) BO 3 sts, work 9 sts, join a second ball of yarn and BO center 20 sts, work to end. Working both sides at same time, BO 3 sts at beginning of next row, then 4 sts at beginning of next 4 rows, and AT THE SAME TIME, BO 2 sts at each neck once, then decrease 1 st at each neck edge once.

RIGHT FRONT

Using smaller needle and A, CO 35 sts.

Row 1: K1, *k1, yo; repeat from * to last st, k1—68 sts.

Row 2: Knit, dropping yo's—35 sts remain.

Rows 3 and 4: Repeat Rows 1 and 2.

"Punk is really about freedom of expression, TO TAKE THE NORM AND MAKE IT INTO SOMETHING THAT IS YOUR OWN. Something original and non-conformist. Something unique. I think knitting lends itself to the punk aesthetic very well because it lets you take a basic idea and trip it out into what makes you, well, YOU." —NICOLE G., FARMINGTON, MN

ESTABLISH PATTERN

Row 5: K1, [k1, yo] 3 times, pm, knit to last 3 sts, pm, [yo, k1] twice, k1—40 sts.

Row 6: Purl, dropping all yo's—35 sts remain.

Repeat Rows 5 and 6 until piece measures 6" from the beginning, ending with a WS row.

SHAPE BODY

Note: Unravel all dropped sts down to CO row.

(RS) K1, [k1, yo] 3 times, k11, drop next st, k2, drop next st, k13, [yo, k1] twice, k1—38 sts. Purl 1 row, dropping all yo's—33 sts remain. Work even until piece measures 9" from the beginning, ending with a WS row.

(RS) K1, [k1, yo] 3 times, k14, drop next st, k11, [yo, k1] twice, k1—37 sts. Purl 1 row, dropping all yo's—32 sts remain. Work even until piece measures 12" from the beginning, ending with a WS row.

(RS) K1, [k1, yo] 3 times, k17, drop next st, k2, drop next st, k4, [yo, k1] twice, k1—35 sts. Purl 1 row, dropping all yo's—30 sts remain. Work even until armhole measures 6 3/4", ending with a WS row—23 sts remain.

SHAPE NECK AND SHOULDER

(RS) BO 3 sts at neck edge twice, 2 sts twice, then decrease 1 st every other row twice and, AT THE SAME TIME, when piece measures same as for Back to shoulder shaping, shape shoulder as for Back.

LEFT FRONT

Work as for Right Front, reversing all shaping and dropped st pattern.

FINISHING

Block all pieces to measurements. Sew shoulder seam. Weave in all loose ends.

ARMHOLE EDGING

RS facing, using larger circ needle and 2 strands of B held together, beginning at underarm, pick up and knit 32 sts to shoulder seam, then 32 sts to underarm—64 sts. Begin Garter st (knit every row). Work even for 7 rows. BO all sts loosely. Sew side seams. *Optional: If you prefer, you may sew the side seams first and, using a 16" circ needle, work the Armhole Edging in-the-round (knit 1 rnd, purl 1 rnd).*

BODY EDGING

RS facing, using larger circ needle and 2 strands of B held together, beginning at bottom of left Front, pick up and knit 25 sts along left Front CO edge, 53 sts along Back CO edge, and 25 sts along right Front CO edge—103 sts. Work as for Armhole Edging.

NECK EDGING

RS facing, using larger circ needle and 2 strands of B held together, beginning at right Front neck edge, after openwork border, pick up and knit 12 sts to shoulder seam, 23 sts across Back neck shaping, and 12 sts to beginning of openwork border—47 sts. Work as for Armhole Edging.

Beginning 12" up from bottom edge, sew large buttons evenly spaced along right Front edge, centered on openwork border, with small buttons on WS as backing. For buttonholes, work each button through one yo in the openwork border along the left Front edge.

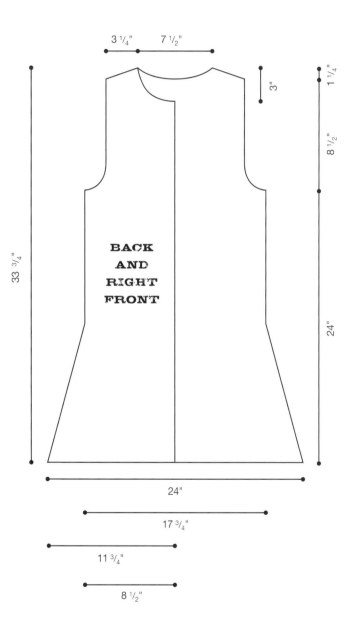

DESIGN/CATHERYN CLARKE

RATING/ARENA

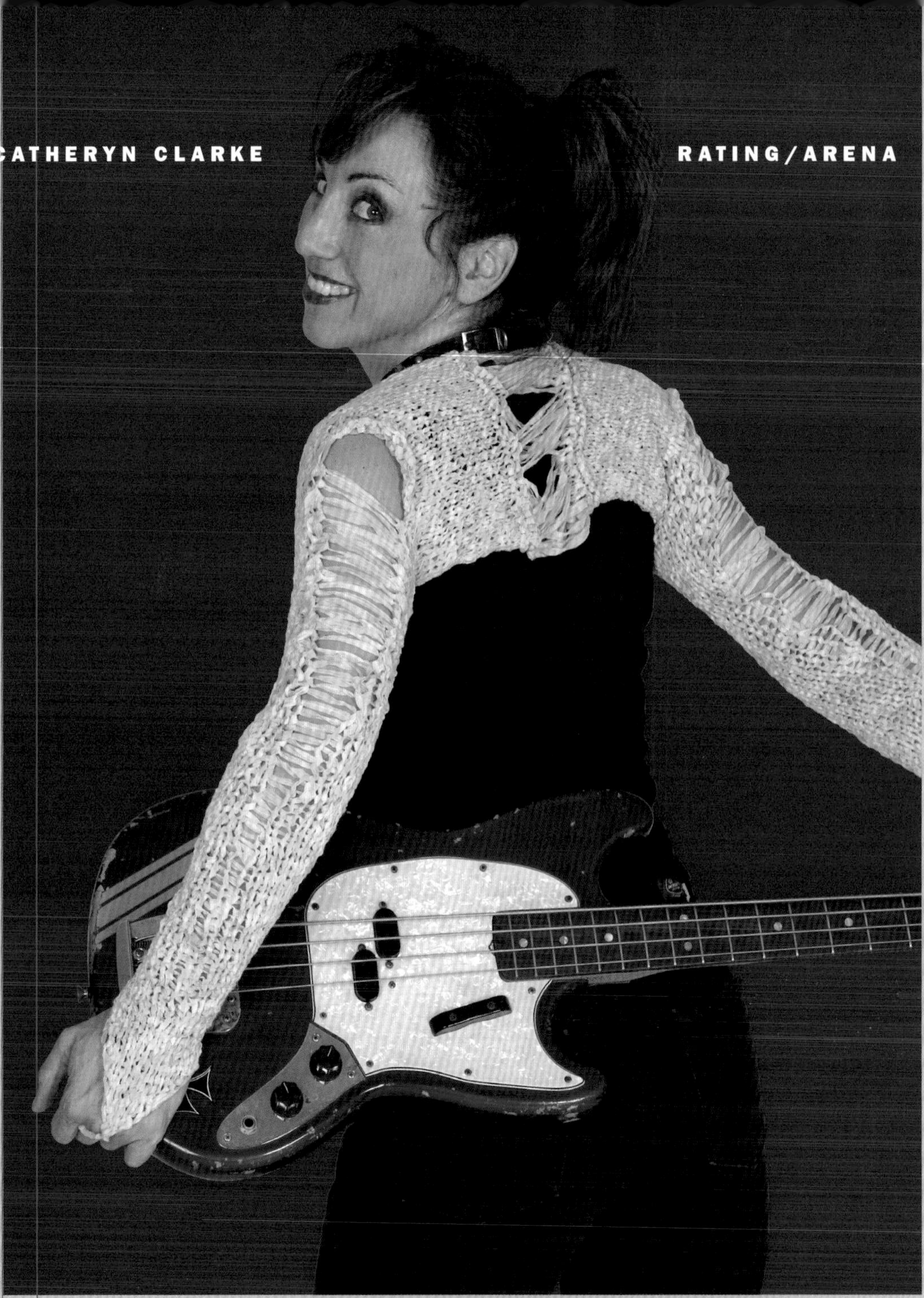

PIXIE SHOULDERETTE

This shoulderette—with its **open yarnovers and criss-crossed back**—is full of elegance and fun, quirky, flattering style. With all of those open spaces, it's also a great piece for showing off your tattoos. It's easier than you might think to knit and **works up fast.**

SIZES

One size fits most

FINISHED MEASUREMENTS

58" cuff to cuff
14" crossback

MATERIALS

Yarn

Crystal Palace Yarns Deco-Ribbon (70% acrylic / 30% nylon; 80 yards / 50 grams): 4 skeins #9235 lemonade

Needles

One pair straight needles size US 11 (8 mm)
Change needle size if necessary to obtain correct gauge.

Notions

Crochet hook size US H/8 (5 mm)
Stitch markers, row markers, cable needle (cn)

GAUGE

13 sts and 16 rows = 4" (10 cm) in Stockinette st (St st)

The Pixie Shoulderette **IS KNIT FROM FINGER TO FINGER** and is an incredibly versatile wardrobe piece!

NOTES

Only one size is given as the fabric is quite stretchy. Notes are included for a wider Back; Sleeve length and width may be altered by adding rows of Stockinette st between the ladders or extra edge sts as desired. In this case, purchase an extra skein of yarn to be safe.

When casting on and binding off, leave a 15" tail. This will be used to crochet the "finger loop" for each hand.

Ladders are formed throughout the pattern by making yarnovers (yo's) on a series of rows, and dropping the yo's on every subsequent row.

Yo2, yo3, and yo4: Bring yarn between needles to front, wrap yarn over right-hand needle from front to back; continue to wrap as many times as indicated. The greater the number of wraps, the wider the ladder will be once the yo's are dropped.

SHOULDERETTE

LEFT SLEEVE

CO 2 sts, leaving a 15" tail for finishing. Begin St st, increase 1 st each side every other row 8 times, ending with a WS row—18 sts.

BEGIN LADDERS

Row 1 (RS): K9, yo, k9.
Row 2: P9, drop yo from previous row, yo, p9.
Rows 3–14: Repeat Rows 1 and 2—piece should measure 7" from the beginning. Place marker (pm) after st #9 on Row 14.

SHAPE SLEEVE

Row 15 (Inc Row): K1, m1, knit to marker, drop yo from previous row, yo, knit to last st, m1, k1—20 sts.

Row 16: Purl to marker, drop yo from previous row, yo, purl to end.

Rows 17–22: Repeat Rows 15 and 16—26 sts after Row 21.

Row 23: Knit to marker, drop yo from previous row, yo, knit to end.

Row 24: Purl to marker, drop yo from previous row, yo, purl to end.

Rows 25–34: Repeat Rows 23 and 24—piece should measure 11 3/4" from the beginning.

SHAPE UPPER ARM

Row 35 (RS): Knit to marker, drop yo from previous row, yo2, knit to end.

Row 36: Purl to marker, drop yo's from previous row, yo2, purl to end.

Row 37: K1, m1, knit to 2 sts before marker, ssk, drop yo's from previous row, yo2, k2tog, knit to last st, m1, k1.

Row 38: Repeat Row 36.

Rows 39–40: Repeat Rows 35 and 36.

Row 41: Knit to marker, drop yo's from previous row, yo3, knit to end.

Row 42: Purl to marker, drop yo's from previous row, yo3, purl to end.

Rows 43–44: Repeat Rows 41 and 42.

Row 45: K1, m1, knit to 2 sts before marker, ssk, drop yo's from previous row, yo3, k2tog, knit to last st, m1, k1.

Row 46: Repeat Row 42.

Rows 47–50: Repeat Rows 41 and 42.

Row 51: Knit to marker, drop yo's from previous row, yo4, knit to end.

Row 52: Purl to marker, drop yo's from previous row, yo4, purl to end.

Row 53: K1, m1, knit to 2 sts before marker, ssk, drop yo's from previous row, yo4, k2tog, knit to last st, m1, k1.

Row 54: Repeat Row 52.

Rows 55–58: Repeat Rows 51 and 52.

Row 59: Repeat Row 53.

Row 60: Repeat Row 52.

Row 61 (Inc Row): K1, m1, knit to marker, yo4, knit to last st, m1, k1—28 sts.

Row 62: Repeat Row 52.

Rows 63–68: Repeat Rows 51 and 52.

Row 69 (Inc Row): Repeat Row 61—30 sts.

Row 70: Repeat Row 52.

Rows 71–74: Repeat Rows 51 and 52; remove marker after last row.

Place row marker each side for Sleeve. Piece should measure 21" from the beginning.

BACK

Row 75: K15, CO 10 sts, k15—40 sts.

Row 76: K3, pm, p37, pm, k3.

Row 77: Knit.

Row 78: K3, p37, k3.

Rows 79–96: Repeat Rows 76 and 77—piece should measure approximately 26 1/2" from the beginning.

Note: For increased Back width, work extra rows here and on the other side of the Criss-Cross Pattern where indicated; add 2 extra rows on each side (4 rows total) for every additional inch desired.

Rows 97–99: Knit, removing stitch markers on last row.

12 1/4"

RIGHT
SLEEVE

BACK

LEFT
SLEEVE

58"

14"

22"

CO edge

●●
1/2"

CRISS-CROSS PATTERN

Note: See Criss-Cross Pattern (Up Close) on pages 114–115 for a tutorial on Rows 100 and 101.

Row 100 (WS): *K1, wrapping yarn 6 times; repeat from * across. Do not turn work. Carefully slip sts back to left-hand needle, dropping all yo's. You now have a series of oversized loops hanging from the left-hand needle. Place work on a flat surface, with needle point facing to the right. Remove needle. *Note: The following criss-crosses will be worked without knitting any of the sts.* **Separate (nudge) your sts into groups of 4 sts each. Starting from right-hand side, cross the first group of 4 sts in back of the second group of 4 sts and place back on needle. Repeat from ** 4 times until all sts have been transferred to right-hand needle. Turn work.

Row 101 (RS): Knit 1 row, working each st very loosely, and pulling the work after each st so that the crossed loops are all the same length and do not pull in or buckle.

Rows 102–103: Knit.

Row 104: K3, pm, p37, pm, k3.

Row 105: Knit.

Row 106: K3, p37, k3.

Rows 107–124: Repeat Rows 105 and 106, removing markers on last row.

Note: If you added extra rows for a wider Back before working the Criss-Cross Pattern, add the same number of rows here.

Row 125: K15, pm, BO 10 sts, k15—30 sts remain. Place row marker each side for Sleeve.

Note: The BO sts create a large gap, but the multiple yo's and dropped sts worked over the next few rows will bridge the gap.

RIGHT SLEEVE

Work as for left Sleeve, in reverse order, beginning at Row 74 and working back to Row 1 (beginning of Sleeve shaping), substituting the following Dec Rows for the same numbered Inc Rows:

Rows 69 and 61 (Dec Row): K1, ssk, knit to marker, yo4, knit to last 3 sts, k2tog, k1—26 sts remain after Row 61.

Rows 21, 19, 17, and 15 (Dec Row): K1, ssk, knit to marker, drop yo from previous row, yo, knit to last 3 sts, k2tog, k1—18 sts remain after Row 15.

FINISH LADDERS

Row 1 (WS): P9, drop yo from previous row, yo, p9.

Row 2: K9, yo, k9.

Rows 3–14: Repeat Rows 1 and 2.

Row 15: Purl.

Row 16: K2tog, purl to last 2 sts, k2tog—16 sts remain.

Rows 17–28: Repeat Rows 15 and 16—4 sts remain after Row 28.

Row 29: [K2tog] twice—2 sts remain.

BO last 2 sts purlwise, leaving 15" tail for crochet chain loop.

FINISHING

Using crochet hook and BO tail, work crochet chain 3" long, or long enough to reach around middle finger and back to BO edge. Fasten off. Sew end of chain to BO edge at beginning of chain. Weave in ends. Repeat for CO edge. Beginning 4" up from CO and BO edges, sew Sleeve seams to markers. Weave in all loose ends.

CRISS-CROSS PATTERN (UP CLOSE)

Here's a tutorial to help you understand how to work the Criss-Cross Pattern that runs across the back of the Shoulderette (Rows 100 and 101). In these photos, the criss-crosses are worked on a swatch. In the Shoulderette, you are working with more stitches (thus you are working more criss-crosses).

Do not turn work. This is what the row will look like after you have done all of the wraps.

STEP 1: Row 100 (WS): *K1, wrapping yarn around the needle 6 times (instead of once as is standard) before lifting the stitch off the left-hand needle; repeat from * across. The photo on the left shows what your knitting will look like after you have done the wrapping and when you are in the process of lifting the stitch off the left-hand needle.

You will now have a bunch of giant loops hanging off one needle.

STEP 2: Without knitting the stitches, slip the stitches off the needle and back onto the left-hand needle, dropping all of the yarnovers (the wrapped yarn). The photo on the left shows the first two stitches being slipped.

114

STEP 3: Place needle with stitches on a work surface, with needle pointing to the right. Remove needle.

In this photo you can see two groups of stitches crossed.

STEP 4: Separate (nudge) your stitches into individual groups of 4 stitches each. Because the stitches are so big, they are easy to manipulate. Starting from the right-hand side, cross the first group of 4 stitches in back of the second group of 4 stitches and transfer to the right-hand needle. Repeat to end.

After you knit the next row, the criss-crosses will look like this.

Row 101: Carefully knit the next row very loosely. It's going to look pretty messy at this point. Don't worry.

NEW WAVE TIE

This pattern is a nice **alternative for beginner knitters** who don't want to make another scarf but still want to keep their endeavors simple.

INSPIRATION: THE CARS

New wave. New punk. The Cars brought music fame to Boston. Ric Ocasek and company oozed hit after hit—ties intact, nary a drop of sweat on their brows.

FINISHED MEASUREMENTS

3 ³/₄" wide at widest point x 57" long

MATERIALS

Yarn

Lucy Neatby Celestial Merino (100% premium merino wool; 175 yards / 50 grams): 1 ball #G02 lime

Needles

One pair straight needles size US 4 (3.5 mm)
Change needle size if necessary to obtain correct gauge.

GAUGE

25 sts and 32 rows = 4" (10 cm) in Garter stitch (knit every row)

KEEP ALL INCREASES AND DECREASES ON THE SAME SIDE (WS). The finished Tie will look nicer if they're hidden.

TIE

CO 3 sts. Begin Garter st (knit every row). Work even for 2 rows.
Next row (RS): K1-f/b, k1, k1-f/b—5 sts.
(WS) Continuing in Garter st, increase one st each side every other row 9 times, ending with a RS row—23 sts.

TIE BODY

Dec Row 1 (WS): K2tog, knit to last 2 sts. k2tog—21 sts remain.
Work even until piece measures 7" from the beginning, ending with a RS row.
Note: The increases and decreases through this point in the pattern are placed at the beginning and end of the rows to make a sharp angle. Remaining decreases are placed 2 stitches from each side to keep edges smooth.
*Dec Row 2 (WS): K2, k2tog, knit to last 4 sts, k2tog, k2—19 sts remain.
Work even for 35 rows. (Note: For a longer or shorter Tie, add or subtract rows in this section.)
Repeat from * 6 times—7 sts remain.

NARROW END OF TIE

Work even until piece measures approximately 62" or desired length from the beginning, ending with a RS row.
(WS) K2tog, k3, k2tog—5 sts remain. Knit 1 row.
(WS) K2tog, k1, k2tog —3 sts remain. Knit 1 row. BO all sts.

FINISHING

Weave in all loose ends. Block gently.

RATING / GARAGE

MOTOR CITY ARM WARMERS

Arm warmers are a staple in the wardrobe of any punk rocker, scenester, artist, or bohemian lifestyler. Wear these with jeans, wear 'em onstage, paint in 'em, play guitar in 'em, **ride your motorcycle in 'em.** They are versatile and, best of all, they actually keep you warm! While this is a simple pattern, because of the fine yarn and small needles, **these can take a little bit of time** to make, so be patient.

INSPIRATION: THE STOOGES

The godfathers of punk and garage rock, Iggy and company had the songs and the lifestyle that legends are made of.

SIZES

Small/Medium (Large)

FINISHED MEASUREMENTS

5 (6)" wrist circumference (unstretched)
15" arm length

MATERIALS

Yarn

Rowan Wool/Cotton (50% merino wool / 50% cotton;
123 yards / 50 grams):
Solid Version: 2 balls #943 flower (A)
Striped Version: 1 ball each #908 black (A), #946 elf
(B), and #959 Bilberry fool (C)

Needles

One pair straight needles size US 3 (3.25 mm)
Change needle size if necessary to obtain correct
gauge.

Notions

Crochet hook size US D/3 (3.25 mm) (optional)
Tapestry needle; row counter (optional)

GAUGE

35 sts and 25 rows = 4" (10 cm) in 2x2 Rib

2 X 2 RIB

(multiple of 4 sts; 1-row repeat)
All Rows: *K2, p2; repeat from * across.

Stripe Sequence

14 rows A, 8 rows B, 4 rows C, 2 rows B, 10 rows A,
4 rows B, 10 rows C, 4 rows B, 10 rows A, 2 rows B,
4 rows C, 8 rows B, 14 rows A

NOTES

Binding off must be done loosely to ensure comfort in wearing.

Arm Warmers may be lengthened and worn "scrunched up" on
your arms. For this option, additional yarn may be required.

ARM WARMERS

CUFF

SOLID VERSION

Using A, CO 44 (52) sts. Begin 2x2 Rib. Work even in pattern until piece measures 15" or desired length from the beginning. BO all sts loosely in pattern.

STRIPED VERSION

Using A, CO 44 (52) sts. Begin 2x2 Rib and Stripe Sequence. Work even in pattern until Stripe Sequence is complete. BO all sts loosely in pattern.

FINISHING

RS's facing, sew side seam, beginning at cast-on edge and ending 2 1/2" from bound-off edge. Leaving a gap of approximately 1 1/2" for thumbhole, rejoin yarn and sew side seam to end. Using crochet hook, work 1 row single crochet around thumb opening for a neater finish (optional). Weave in all ends.

KNIT BOTH ARM WARMERS AT THE SAME TIME ON ONE SET OF NEEDLES. This helps you keep track of the striping progression and keeps them the same length.

"TO ME THERE IS NOTHING MORE PUNK ROCK THAN MAKING YOUR OWN CLOTHES.

You get to design them YOUR way, to YOUR taste, in YOUR exact size, creating totally unique pieces. No one will ever own a sweater exactly like yours! I dye my own yarn and make up my own patterns because I want to stand out from the crowd. It's not just another store-bought, trendy scarf made by starving children in impoverished countries— it's a Kool-Aid rainbow scarf made on my own needles, full of screw-ups and drop stitches but it still looks damn good. It has character. "—LIZZY C., SAN FRANCISCO, CA

RATING/NIGHTCLUB

LONDON'S BURNIN' STRAP

Strong enough to withstand the weight of an electric guitar, this quick-knit **strap is a must.** Felt it to your desired size. Make it with or without polka dots. And remember—play your guitar loud!

INSPIRATION: THE CLASH

One of punk's seminal bands, The Clash was full of passion, politics, and amazing pop melodies. Joe Strummer, their guitarist, was a legend who led the way for many musicians to follow.

FINISHED MEASUREMENTS

Short (Long) Strap

4 1/2" wide x 60 (70)" long before felting; 3 1/2" x 50 (60)" after felting

MATERIALS

Yarn

Reynolds Lopi (100% Icelandic wool; 109 yards / 100 grams): 1 skein each #059 black (MC) and #0910 fuchsia (CC)

Needles

One pair straight needles size US 13 (9 mm)
Change needle size if necessary to obtain correct gauge.

Notions

Yarn bobbins (optional)

GAUGE

10 sts and 13 rows = 4" (10 cm) in Stockinette stitch (St st) (before felting)

NOTES

Don't worry if Strap measurements vary slightly; length will be adjusted during the felting process.

To avoid tangling yarns, wind CC onto bobbins, if desired, for individual polka dots.

To aid in Finishing, cut CC after each polka dot and weave in ends. Do not carry floats along back of strap, as this may cause puckering and distort felted fabric.

STRAP

Using MC, CO 3 sts.
Row 1 (RS): K1-f/b, k1, k1-f/b—5 sts.
Row 2 and all WS rows: Purl.
Row 3: K1-f/b, k3, k1-f/b—7 sts.
Row 5: K1-f/b, k5, k1-f/b—9 sts.
Row 7: K1-f/b, k7, k1-f/b—11 sts.
Row 9: K1-f/b, k9, k1-f/b—13 sts.

BEGIN POLKA DOTS

(WS) Begin Row 1 of Chart. Work entire Chart 9 (11) times. (Strap should measure approximately 56 (66)" from the beginning.)

Continuing in MC, work even for 5 rows, ending with a RS row.

SHAPE END

Row 1 (WS): P2tog, p9, p2tog—11 sts remain.
Row 2 and all RS rows: Knit.
Row 3: P2tog, p7, p2tog—9 sts remain.
Row 5: P2tog, p5, p2tog—7 sts remain.
Row 7: P2tog, p3, p2tog—5 sts remain.
Row 9: P2tog, p1, p2tog—3 sts remain.
BO all sts.

FINISHING

Weave in all loose ends. Place completed Strap in a zippered pillowcase. Using hot water and a very small amount of detergent, add to the washing machine with a pair of jeans or tennis shoes for good agitation, and felt to desired size. Mine took three washes, so be patient! When felting is complete, rinse Strap in cold water and spin out excess water using the machine's Spin cycle. Remove and shape as necessary, pulling the Strap into desired shape.

Use scissors to punch holes in "triangles;" attach the Strap to your guitar.

KEY

 A   B

Note: Chart is worked in St st—knit on RS, purl on WS

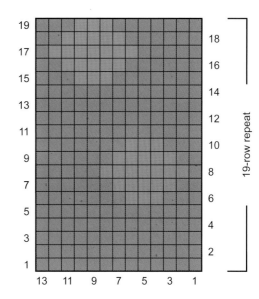

19-row repeat

IF YOU MOVE AROUND LIKE A MANIAC ON STAGE, sew leather triangles over the shaped ends of the Strap and then punch the holes to attach the Strap to your guitar. This will reinforce the Strap and make it punk-worthy.

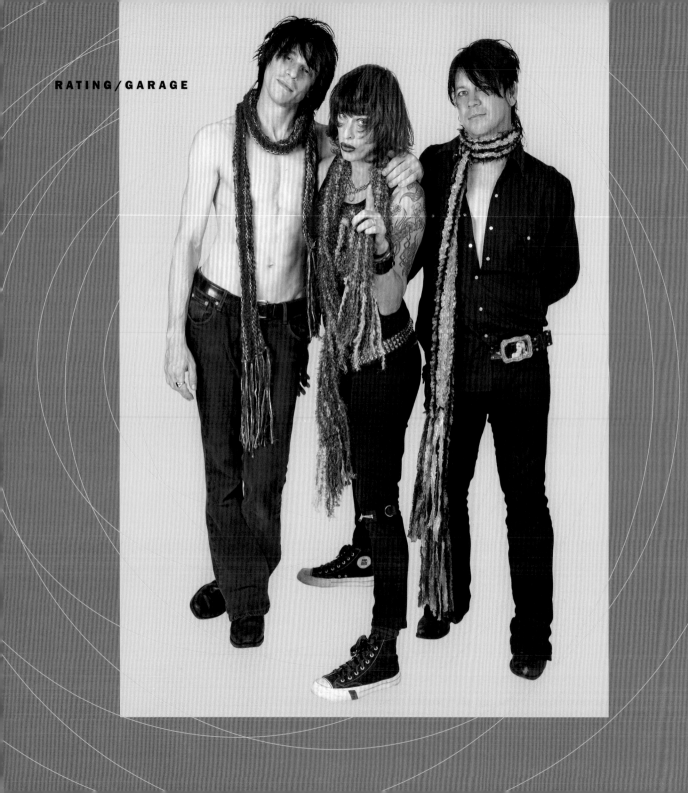

FLYING V SCARF

This is a **great beginner scarf.** To start, you cast on a lot of stitches—enough for the length of the scarf—then you only need to knit a few rows to achieve the width. You can make this scarf a thousand unique ways by **experimenting with different yarns.** I've made it three ways here to suit three musical personalities!

FINISHED MEASUREMENTS

Approximately 98 1/2" wide x 4 1/2" long (Version 2 is 5 1 1/4" wide), before Fringe

MATERIALS

Yarn

Version 1

Crystal Palace Yarns Rave (100% nylon; 44 yards / 50 grams): 1 ball each #311 raving red (A), #301 outrage orange (B), and #302 pacifier pink (C)
Crystal Palace Whisper (100% microfiber; 97 yards / 50 grams): 2 balls #2843 black (D)

Version 2

Crystal Palace Yarns Punk (75% nylon / 25% polyester; 55 yards / 50 grams): 1 ball each #5096 anime lime (A) and #5099 posh pink (B)

Version 3

Debbie Bliss Soho (100% wool; 77 yards / 50 grams): 2 balls #02 browns/earthtones (A)
Berroco Quest Colors (100% nylon; 82 yards / 50 grams): 1 ball #9935 aesthete (B)
GGH Relax (32% wool / 32% nylon / 26% acrylic / 10% alpaca; 120 yards / 50 grams): 1 ball #07 army green (C)

Needles

One 32" (80 cm) long circular (circ) needle size US 13 (9 mm), or longer if desired
Change needle size if necessary to obtain correct gauge.

Notions

Crochet hook size US M/13 (9 mm) for Fringe

GAUGE

6 1/2 sts and 14 rows = 4" (10 cm) in Garter stitch (knit every row)

STRIPE SEQUENCES

All three scarves are knit from the same basic pattern, varying yarn and Stripe Sequence. Use one of the following or create your own!
Version 1: 4 rows A, 2 rows D, 4 rows B, 2 rows D, 4 rows C.
Version 2: 2 rows A, 2 rows B, 2 rows A, 2 rows B, 2 rows A, 2 rows B, 2 rows A, 2 rows B, 2 rows A.
Version 3: 4 rows A, 2 rows B, 4 rows C, 2 rows B, 4 rows A.

Previous page (from left to right): Version 3, Version 2, Version 1

NOTE

For Version 1 only, use 2 strands of D held together.

SCARF

Using A, CO 160 sts. Begin Garter st (knit every row) and Stripe Sequence of your choice. Work even until Stripe Sequence is complete. BO all sts loosely.

FINISHING
Weave in all ends.

FRINGE
Cut 24" lengths of each yarn for Fringe. Using crochet hook, work Fringe (see page 135) along both ends of Scarf and wear with rock 'n' roll pride.

With such a long CO row, **IT'S IMPORTANT TO KEEP YOUR CO STITCHES VERY LOOSE!** You might want to CO with a needle 1 or 2 sizes larger than required for the rest of the pattern.

Version 1

129

ABOUT THE MODELS

Everyone in this book is involved in the rock 'n' roll scene in Los Angeles in some way—from playing in a band to doing hair for rockers, to writing reviews, to taking band photos. They all contribute to the underground heartbeat of Hollywood and I hope you will check out their Web sites for more info about them!

Annathena Grigelevich
Annathena is a professional DJ and self-described "music geek." With a long list of credits to back up her ragin' reputation, she's one of the busiest rock DJs in Hollywood. When she isn't spinning she enjoys listening to '70s glitter records, chewing gum, writing, and playing pinball. **www.missannathena.com**

Apollo Staar
Photographer, indie filmmaker, DJ, and all-around scenester, Apollo adds flair and style to everything he touches.
www.myspace.com/apollostarr

Calico Cooper
Born on a tour bus, Calico has lived an exciting, passionate life. She says she lives for rock music, sunrises, and peanut butter. With eight world tours and four films under her belt, she wants to conquer all other genres of entertainment and show them who's boss! **www.calicocooper.com**

Casper
Writer, artist, debutante, and bassist in Coyote Shivers' band, Casper's motto is, "Too beautiful to live, too tough to die."
www.myspace.com/casperstar

Cheryl Sale (aka Rock 'n' Roll Cheryl)
A native Californian, Cheryl is a hairstylist at Giuseppe Franco in Beverly Hills. Most of her clients are in the music industry and are also her friends. **www.rocknrollcheryl.com**

Coyote Shivers
Coyote is a movie star, rock 'n' roll star, DJ, and sex symbol. **www.coyoteshivers.com**

Jeremy White
Jeremy is the lead vocalist, songwriter, and harmonica player for the rootsy rock 'n' roll band The Blessings. **www.theblessingsweb.com**

Jo Almeida
Jo played guitar for The Dogs D'Amour and currently plays everything with strings on it for country singer Chris Richards. He is also a fine artist.
www.home.earthlink.net/~joalmeida/

Johnny 99
Johnny 99 is the bassist of punk-fueled power-pop rock act Silver Needle. He is also the founder of LA's emerging kiss-or-kill scene, a community of artists fusing punk, power pop, and rock 'n' roll with high-energy stage antics. **www.silver-needle.com**

Kastle

Kastle is a nice grrrl from Texas who came to Hollywood with a mohawk and big dreams. Fueled by rock 'n' roll, she reached her goal of becoming a reporter and editor for the *Los Angeles Times*. Read about her latest adventures in her column for www.coolgrrrls.com and in travel books, including Fodor's and Best Places. **www.coolgrrrls.com**

Kourtney Klein

Kourtney started her career as a band nerd, playing orchestral percussion and jazz in school. She can now be found playing drum sets in the back of the alternative hard rock threesome Drama Addict. **www.dramaaddict.com**

Lesli Matta

A former Miss Boston, Lesli is a singer-songwriter, drummer, guitarist, piano player, fashion designer, and TV personality. **www.wickedqueen.com**

Leslita Neptuna

Leslita Neptuna (Leslie Anne Burnet) hails from Oklahoma and is the mother of Paul William. Besides playing guitar with The Neptunas, Leslita moonlights as the female vocalist in Order of the Wand, which also features her husband, Dallas Don. **www.theneptunas.com**

Megan McCarter

A guitarist and singer-songwriter, Megan enjoys scary movies, pizza, antiques, and long walks on the beach with her dog, Beatrice. **www.myspace.com/meganplaysguitar**

Pamita Neptuna

Pamita still manhandles the bass and shouts with the Neptunas but also plays with an all-girl country combo called Dime Box Band and the world's only all-female Cheap Trick tribute band, Cheap Chick. **www.theneptunas.com**

Roy Mayorga

A drummer and composer, Roy has played for Nausea, Thorn, Crisis, Soul Fly, Ozzy, and Dave Navarro. He is currently doing film soundtracks and session work. **www.myspace.com/royfilmscore**

Sienna Degovia

Sienna is "lead cupcake" and bassist of the Randies. **www.therandies.com**

Texas Terri

An underground legend in the punk rock 'n' roll world, Texas Terri hails from Austin, Texas, but lives in Hollywood. More than just a wild and extremely entertaining front person, Texas Terri also writes the songs for her band. **www.texasterri.com**

ABOUT THE DESIGNERS

Lisi Grinstein is the owner and lead personality at the Stitch Cafe in Valley Village, California. She designs with both knitting needles and crochet hooks and has taught countless people the fiber crafts. Her designs are all over her shop, and she is a walking enyclopedia of knit style know-how!
www.stitchcafe.com

Catheryn Clarke taught herself to knit and immediately started to create her own patterns. She knits and designs in a very unique punk/goth fashion and lives in Hollywood with her rock 'n' roll partner in crime, Hornby, and her faithful cat, Lord Byron. Follow her tales of yarn madness at her blog:
www.arakneknits.typepad.com

Mary Delfin lives in Australia and loves punk music. Her motto is that if she cannot knit it, she knits around it. Read more about her crazy life at "Confessions of a Knitting Ninja":
www.kalenture.blogspot.com

"ROCK 'N' ROLL IS A PURE REACTION TO THE WORLD.
Music celebrates individual identity and relishes in the human soul. KNITTING IS A CRAFT DONE BY THE PATIENT AND CREATIVE. The thought process of hand-crafting a piece with love and attention to detail is similar to that of songwriting. Both take vision and passion to create a unique piece that is a reflection of the artist's identity." —JOHNNY 99

RECOMMENDED READING

In addition to the reference books on page 12, I recommend the following:

Weekend Knitting: 50 Unique Projects and Ideas by Melanie Falick—for terrific, quick-to-knit patterns

Hollywood Knits: 30 Original Suss Designs by Suss Cousins—beautiful patterns

At Knit's End: Meditations for Women Who Knit Too Much by Stephanie Pearl-McPhee—great read

Simple Knits with a Twist: Unique Projects for Creative Knitters by Erika Knight—pure inspiration

Loop-d-Loop: More than 40 Novel Designs for Knitters by Teva Durham—incredibly imaginative

Maggie's Ireland: Designer Knits on Location by Maggie Jackson—Wow. Check out her way of knitting with several different types of yarns all tied together.

Knitorama by Rachel Matthews—knit your cake!

Alterknits: Imaginative Projects and Creativity Exercises by Leigh Radford—fantastic projects

YARN SUPPLIERS

If you can't find the yarns called for in the patterns in this book in your LYS, contact these distributors and manufacturers.

Artemis Exquisite Embellishments
(Distributes Hannah Silk Ribbon)
5155 Myrtle Avenue
Eureka, CA 95503
888-233-5187
www.artemisinc.com

Berroco, Inc
14 Elmdale Road
PO Box 367
Uxbridge, MA 01569
508-278-2527
www.berroco.com

Brown Sheep Company, Inc
100662 County Road 16
Mitchell, NE 69357
800-826-9136
www.brownsheep.com

Cascade
PO Box 58168
Tukwila, WA 98138
800-548-1048
www.cascadeyarns.com

Classic Elite Yarns, Inc
122 Western Avenue
Lowell, MA 01851
978-453-2837
www.classiceliteyarns.com

Crystal Palace Yarns
160 23rd Street
Richmond, CA 94804
510-237-9988
www.straw.com

JCA, Inc
(Distributes Reynolds and
Adrienne Vittadini)
35 Scales Lane
Townsend, MA 04169
978-597-8794
www.jcacrafts.com

Karabella Yarns, Inc
1201 Broadway
New York, NY 10001
212-684-2665
www.karabellayarns.com

Knit One, Crochet Too, Inc
91 Tandberg Trail, Unit 6
Windham, ME 04062
207-892-9625
www.knitonecrochettoo.com

Knitting Fever, Inc
(Distributes Debbie Bliss, Online,
Sirdar, and Katia)
35 Debevoise Avenue
Roosevelt, NY 11575
www.knittingfever.com

Lucy Neatby
45 Dorothea Drive
Dartmouth, NS B2W 5X4
Canada
866-272-7796
www.tradewindknits.com

Muench Yarns, Inc
(Distributes GGH)
1323 Scott Street
Petaluma, CA 94954
707-763-9377
www.muenchyarns.com

Needful Yarns, Inc
(Distributes Filtes King)
60 Industrial Parkway PMB #233
Cheektowaga, NY 14227
416.398.3700
www.needfulyarnsinc.com

Russi Sales, Inc
(Distributes Fonty)
605 Clark Road
Bellingham, WA 98225
www.russisales.com

S. R. Kertzer Limited
(Distributes Baby Monkey)
50 Trowers Road
Woodbridge, ON L4L 7K6
Canada
800-263-2354
www.kertzer.com

Tahki Stacy Charles, Inc
(Distributes Filatura Di Crosa)
8000 Cooper Avenue
Building 1
Glendale, NY 11385
800-338-YARN
www.tahkistacycharles.com

Unicorn Books and Crafts
(Distributes Lana Grossa)
1388 Ross Street
Petaluma, CA 94954
800-289-9276
www.unicornbooks.com

Unique Kolours
(Distributes Colinette)
1428 Oak Lane
Downington, PA 19335
800-25-2DYE4
www.colinette.com

Westminster Fibers
(Distributes Rowan)
4 Townsend West, Unit 8
Nashua, NH 03063
www.knitrowan.com

BASIC ABBREVIATIONS

BO – Bind off

Ch – Chain

Circ – Circular

CO – Cast on

Dc (double crochet) – Working from right to left, yarn over hook (2 loops on hook), insert hook into the next stitch, yarn over hook and pull up a loop (3 loops on hook), [yarn over and draw through 2 loops] twice.

Dpn – Double-pointed needle(s)

K – Knit

K2tog – Knit 2 sts together.

K3tog – Knit 3 sts together.

K1-f/b – Knit into front loop and back loop of same stitch to increase one stitch.

M1R (make 1-right slanting) – With the tip of the left-hand needle inserted from back to front, lift the strand between the two needles onto the left-hand needle; knit it through the front loop to increase one stitch.

M1 or M1L (make 1-left slanting) – With the tip of the left-hand needle inserted from front to back, lift the strand between the two needles onto the left-hand needle; knit the strand through the back loop to increase one stitch.

M1P (make 1 purlwise) - With the tip of the left-hand needle inserted from back to front, lift the strand between the two needles onto the left-hand needle; purl the strand through the front loop to increase one stitch.

P – Purl

P2tog – Purl 2 sts together.

P1-f/b – Purl the next st through the front of its loop, then through the back of its loop, to increase one st.

Pm – Place marker

Rnd – Round

RS – Right side

Sc (single crochet) – Insert hook into next st and draw up a loop (2 loops on hook), yarn over and draw through both loops on hook.

Skp – (slip, knit, pass) – Slip next st knitwise to right-hand needle, k1, pass slipped st over knit st.
Sl (slip) – Slip stitch(es) as if to purl, unless otherwise specified. Sl st (crochet slip stitch) – Insert hook in st, yarn over hook, and draw through loop on hook.

Sl st (crochet slip stitch) – Insert hook in st, yarn over hook, and draw through loop on hook.

Sm – Slip marker

Ssk (slip, slip, knit) – Slip the next 2 sts to the right-hand needle one at a time as if to knit; return them back to left-hand needle one at a time in their new orientation; knit them together through the back loop(s).

Ssp (slip, slip, purl) – Slip the next 2 sts to right-hand needle one at a time as if to knit; return them to the left-hand needle one at a time in their new orientation; purl them together through the back loop(s).

St(s) – stitch(es)

K1-tbl – Knit one stitch through the back loop, twisting the stitch.

Tbl – through the back loop

Tog – Together

WS – Wrong side

Yo – Yarnover (see Special Techniques)

SPECIAL TECHNIQUES

Cable CO: Make a loop (using a slip knot) with the working yarn and place it on the left-hand needle (first st CO), knit into slip knot, draw up a loop but do not drop st from left hand needle; place new loop on left-hand needle; *insert the tip of the right-hand needle into the space between the last 2 sts on the left-hand needle and draw up a loop; place the loop on the left-hand needle. Repeat from * for remaining sts to be CO, or for casting on at the end of a row in progress.

Crochet Chain: Make a slip knot and place it on a crochet hook. Holding tail end of yarn in left hand, *take hook under ball end of yarn from front to back; draw yarn on hook back through previous st on hook to form new st. Repeat from * to desired number of sts or length of chain.

Fringe: Using the number of strands required in pattern, fold in half; with RS of piece facing, insert crochet hook just above edge to receive fringe, from back to front; catch the folded strands of yarn with the hook and pull through work to form a loop; insert ends of yarn through loop and pull to tighten.

Garter Stitch: Knit every row when working straight; knit 1 round, purl 1 round when working circular.

Intarsia Colorwork Method: Use a separate length of yarn for each color section; you may wind yarn onto bobbins to make color changes easier. When changing colors, bring the new yarn up and to the right of the yarn just used to twist the yarns and to prevent leaving a hole; do not carry colors not in use across the back of the work.

Reading Charts: Unless otherwise specified in the instructions, when working straight, charts are read from right to left for RS rows, from left to right for WS rows. Row numbers are written at the beginning of each row. Numbers on the right indicate RS rows; numbers on the left indicate WS rows. When working circular, all rounds are read from right to left.

Reverse Stockinette Stitch (Rev St st): Purl on RS rows, knit on WS rows when working straight; purl every round when working circular.

Ribbing: Although rib stitch patterns use different numbers of sts, all are worked in the same way, whether straight (in rows) or circular. The instructions will specify how many sts to knit or purl; the example below uses k1, p1.
Row/Rnd 1: * K1, p1; repeat from * across, (end k1 if an odd number of sts).
Row/Rnd 2: Knit the knit sts and purl the purl sts as they face you.
Repeat Row/Rnd 2 for rib st.

Stockinette Stitch (St st): Knit on RS rows, purl on WS rows when working straight; knit every round when working circular.

Stranded (Fair Isle) Colorwork Method: When more than one color is used per row, carry color(s) not in use loosely across the WS of work. Be sure to secure all colors at beginning and end of rows to prevent holes.

Tassel: Wind yarn 20 times (or to desired thickness) around a piece of cardboard or other object the same length as desired for Tassel. Slide yarn needle threaded with matching yarn under the strands at the top of the tassel; tie tightly, leaving ends long enough for attaching Tassel to garment. Cut through all strands at the opposite end. Tie a second piece of yarn tightly around the Tassel several times, approximately 1/2" from top of Tassel; secure ends inside top of Tassel. Trim ends even; attach to garment.

Yarnover (yo): Bring yarn forward (to the purl position), then place it in position to work the next st. If next st is to be knit, bring yarn over the needle and knit; if next st is to be purled, bring yarn over the needle and then forward again to the purl position and purl. Work the yarnover in pattern on the next row unless instructed otherwise.

ACKNOWLEDGMENTS

My biggest heartfelt thanks to my friend Carol Cutshall, who turned up wearing a scarf that inspired me to knit; to shop owner Lisi Grinstein, who became my good friend and encouraged me to write this book; to my husband, Bam, who wanted a sweater that didn't resemble any sweaters in the shops; and to my mother, who always said I could do anything I put my mind to.

There would be no book without the pursuit of all things creative and for that I credit my husband, Bam. His encouragement, vision, and design input were crucial from the first step to the finished book you are holding, and he never let me give up when it seemed impossible. His support has been unwavering along with his ideas for knitted garments (yes, he provided a lot of input!), which not only amazes me but inspires me. Of course, the fact that he is the photographer helped immensely! Bam, you are my soul mate . . . thank you.

Many of us learn to knit from our moms or grandmothers. My mom didn't knit, although, if her eyesight had been better, I'm sure she would've added knitting to her huge list of creative talents. Her endless belief in my abilities and her positive energy sustained me through many moments of doubt. She was an uplifting influence in my life and even though she didn't live to see the completion of this book, I know she would've been proud. Thank you, Mom, for loving everything I did and for being excited for me!

My dad loves the fact that I took up knitting and he used to out-right giggle about his rock 'n' roll daughter sitting there with yarn and needles. He just couldn't believe it! He taught everyone in our family to think like entrepreneurs and pursue our dreams. Thanks, Dad, for believing in me and for the years of encouragement!

Knitting has a way of bringing people together. A newfound love of yarn strengthened the bond between my friend Catheryn Clarke and me. We quickly discovered we were both searching for designs that were on the punk edge. When talk of a book came up, she was right there to help me overcome my doubts, answer millions of questions, and share her humor along with her amazing designs throughout the book. Catheryn, thank you for rocking so hard and listening to my many "rants"!

Without knitting, I never would have met Lisi Grinstein, who has become a very good friend. She owns The Stitch Cafe in Valley Village, California, and she is the one who planted the seed for this book in the first place. When I complained that there weren't any books with rock 'n' rollers as models, she just looked me squarely in the eye and said, "That's because you're going to write that book, Share." From that moment on, every time I went to her shop (which was and still is often!), she would ask about it. Now there is a real book to talk about, which is so amazing. Thank you for the push, Lisi!

But what is a knitted garment if it is put together badly? Ahh, some of you are nodding your heads right now. Yes, finishing is an art form unto itself. Doing a book with a lot of garments in it and not a lot of time on my hands, I had to rely on an expert finisher who I simply must add is much more than that! Annie Edwards, who worked as a knitwear designer for years, not only sewed together the pieces, she added her design expertise in countless ways, calmly answering my midnight calls (two days before the photo shoot) and encouraging me through the rough spots. Thank you, Annie. You are a lifesaver!

The models were vital to making the book come together the way I pictured it in my head. Rock 'n' roll does have a sense of family, and I felt it when everyone turned up to model for this book. Hugs and Hollywood kisses to all the models!

Way on the outside of my little punk world is my wonderfully patient editor, Melanie Falick. With a voice of calm and strength, she took every call and allayed my fears, again and again! Melanie's strong belief in *Punk Knits,* coupled with her outstanding ability as a knitter, made me feel like I had an army on my side instead of just one woman as an editor. She has become my friend and was a rock throughout the long and unfamiliar process of creating my first book. Thank you for believing in me, Melanie.

To my pals from the old knitting group—Mel, Jessie, Kim and Phyllis—thanks for making me laugh so many nights!

To Karen Krumpza at Needlework Unlimited in Minneapolis, Minnesota, thank you for your friendship and belief in this book from the beginning, and a special thanks for that special afternoon you spent teaching me tricks and tips!

To Amelya Freeman, thank you for helping to get *Punk Knits* out there and fueling the fire!

To my friends and family, thank you for listening over and over when I talked about this knitted piece and that knitted piece. You always seemed interested and excited to hear about all of it: Kat, John, Gary, Jo, Cazza, Ric, Holly, Mum 'n' Dad, Peter, Jo, and all of my pals who wanted knitted items and had to wait for them while I finished this book!

To anyone that I have forgotten, I am just a crazy rock 'n' roller and you know that you're in my heart. So turn up your stereo, pick up some yarn, and start knitting.